The First Beautiful Game

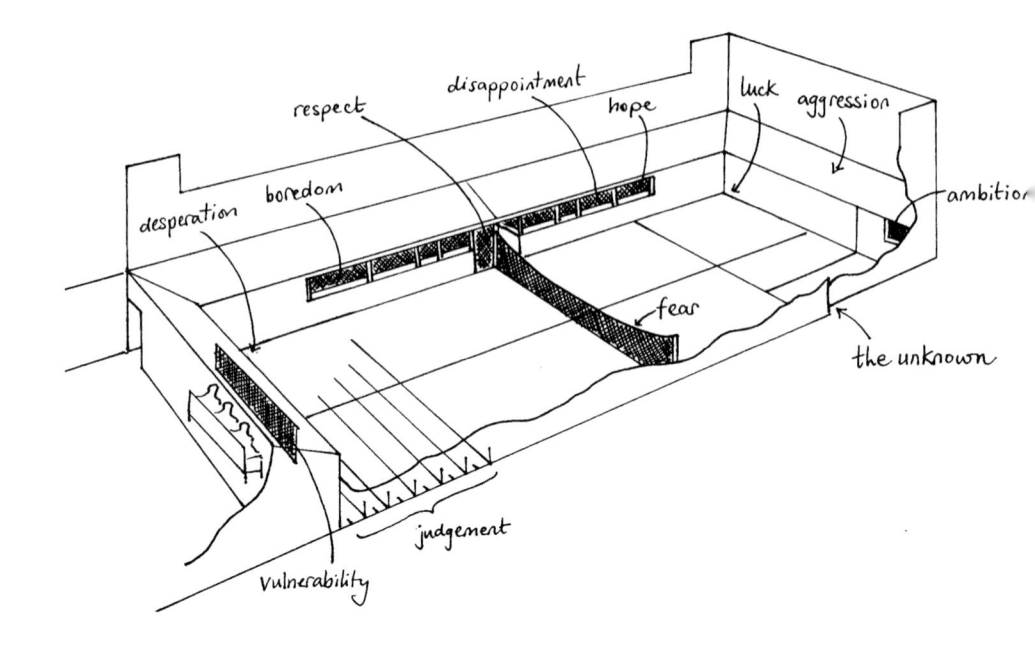

The FIRST BEAUTIFUL GAME

Stories of obsession in Real Tennis

Roman Krznaric

RONALDSON
PUBLICATIONS
2006

First published in 2006 by
Ronaldson Publications
13A Linkside Avenue
Oxford OX2 8HY
www.ronaldsonpublications.com

Copyright © Roman Krznaric 2006

Roman Krznaric asserts the moral right to
be identified as the author of this work.

All rights reserved. No part of this publication may be reproduced, stored in any retrieval system, or transmitted in any form or by any means, electronic, mechanical, photocopying, recording or otherwise, without either the prior permission of the Publisher or a licence permitting restricted copying in the United Kingdom issued by the Copyright Licensing Agency Ltd, 90 Tottenham Court Road, London W1P 9HE.

Cover image: Guillaume Barcellon, tennis professional to Louis XV by Etienne Loys (1753). By permission of the Wimbledon Lawn Tennis Museum.

Frontispiece: *The Court of Experience*, by Kate Raworth, www.kateraworth.com.

Typeset in Centaur.
Cover and book design by Sam Davies.
Printed and bound by the Alden Press, Oxford.

Second printing 2007

1-899804-13-7
978-1-899804-13-9

Contents

Introduction   7
The Wordless Conversation   11
From Abbots to Zealots   31
Life in Court   72
Serving to Gentlemen   100
The Missionary   124
Adventures with my Father   153

Notes   171
References   175
Acknowledgements   179
About the author   181

Introduction

Bent rackets, hand-sewn balls and netted windows. Painted crowns, brass bells and penthouses. Chases, railroads and giraffes. Welcome to the curious world of real tennis. Originating in medieval Europe, the court, rules and equipment have hardly changed in four centuries. Yet this book is not a chronicle of its history, nor is it a manual on technique and strategy. It is about the players and their obsession.

Over the past five years I have spoken with real tennis players about their experiences of the sport, why they play and what it means to them. I learned that most of them are fanatics, some are addicts. More than a few are eccentrics. And I found their stories revealing about the art of living: whether to pursue our passions and ambitions, how to balance work and personal life, why we need respect and equality, where we can find and create beauty. This book tells those stories in their own voices.

I should admit that I am one of the fanatics, an amateur player who has named three bicycles and a car after former World Champions. I first encountered real tennis in the late 1980s when a student. At the time I was dedicated to another sport that, in my ignorance, I called 'tennis' – the game played at Wimbledon and in parks on sunny afternoons. I soon found out two things. First, that real tennis players generally refer to their game as 'tennis' and the modern sport I was familiar with as 'lawn tennis' (a convention followed in this book). Second, that there was no longer much point playing lawn tennis. I was immediately drawn to tennis by its strategic complexity and subtle artistry. There were balls bouncing off the walls and sloping roofs, I had to prevent my opponent from hitting winning targets such as a square with a unicorn painted on it, and I needed to adjust to another unique feature of tennis: that no two courts share precisely the same dimensions and angles.

In the following years I made a third discovery: that tennis was transforming me as a person. It started shaping the way I talked and thought. When speaking with a friend about love, I would instinctively draw an analogy with the game. When contemplating my lack of adventurous spirit, I contrasted it with my spontaneity on court. Gradually tennis became a filter through which I looked at the world and myself. This book is therefore also, unavoidably, about my personal obsession with tennis and how it has shaped my own approach to life.

Two hundred years before football became known as 'the beautiful game,' the French tennis professional Pierre Barcellon, renowned in the late eighteenth century, used the same phrase to describe his own passion.[1] Tennis, as you are about to discover, is the original beautiful game.

*

If you know anything about tennis, it is probably that Henry VIII played at Hampton Court Palace. In fact, in the sixteenth century tennis was played all over Europe and by people of all classes. By the 1970s it had almost completely disappeared. Abandoned courts became used for a bizarre range of activities: amongst them sheep pen and silage storage, part of a prison complex, furniture storeroom, industrial museum, student rooms, synagogue, gymnasium, science laboratory, hotel, squash courts, and garage.[2] Perhaps the most famous former court is the Jeu de Paume, a honey-coloured stone building on the rue de Rivoli near the Louvre in Paris, which now serves as a gallery of contemporary art.

INTRODUCTION

Seek out the tennis courts of the world today and you are unlikely to find many sheep. Old courts are being brought back into use and new ones built. The game has experienced a remarkable revival in the past two decades and there are now some 5,000 players. Most of them play in England, where there are 25 active courts. There are a further 20 courts scattered throughout France, Australia and the United States.

You might imagine that tennis is an elite sport and that the typical English player is someone who went to an exclusive private school and now works in the City of London. He (and it is a he rather than a she) has a posh accent and plays the game more for the social status it bestows than anything else. On court he wears long white flannels and doesn't exert himself too much. Now and then he shouts out 'jolly good shot' to his opponent, although he hates losing.

These are not the kind of people who you will meet in this book. Although tennis has a history of upper-class aficionados, and some of them still inhabit the more traditional clubs, since the 1970s it has become an increasingly middle class sport. Visit a tennis club and you might see a game of doubles between a doctor, a retired plumber, a teacher and an accounts clerk. One of the greatest changes is that you will encounter more women players than in the past, although one club in England and one in the United States still ban women members. There are also over 70 professional tennis players. They are not, however, simply travelling the world playing tournaments like the lawn tennis pros you see on television. The majority work at clubs doing everyday tasks such as giving lessons to their members. While the tournament circuit is growing, there is still not enough money to be earned from competing full-time.

Most of the people I interviewed for this book are club professionals living and working in England. Some are amongst the finest players in the world. I focus on the pros partly because I feel an obligation to dig where I stand. It is astonishing how often we take for granted the people who make our lifestyles possible. We can happily survive without knowing the name of our postman or the chef at our favourite restaurant and what is important in their lives. I had been playing tennis for over a decade before I stopped to think about what life was like for the club professionals who had been teaching me how to play, making the balls, restringing my rackets, umpiring my matches and cleaning the courts. I realised that I had been so busy enjoying the pleasures of playing that I had failed to delve below the surface of my experience. So I decided to speak with the professionals to try to understand tennis from their perspectives.

✻

To begin this journey into the world of tennis I invite you to enter the seating area and take your place with the other spectators.

A tennis court in eighteenth century France.[3]

1 The Wordless Conversation

My fingers curl around the racket handle. I hit the ball firm and straight over the net. He returns it down the centre. I chip the ball to his backhand. His next shot is wide. It strikes the main wall then bounces back into the middle of the court. I move to my right a couple of steps, rotate side-on and flick the ball cross-court. It enters the 'winning gallery,' ringing the brass bell. The sound echoes around the four walls.

I pick up another ball. The warm-up continues, the ball travelling back and forth, the beginning of a wordless conversation that promises intensity, intuition and the unforeseen.

✻

Tennis is the sporting equivalent of the prehistoric tree fern, a survivor from an earlier age that seems to have defied the laws of evolution. The game is still played almost as it was four hundred years ago. And just as the genetic code of the tree fern has revealed to biologists deep secrets of existence, the codes and practices in the ancient sport of tennis contain unexpected insights into the art of living that gradually unfurl through the course of a match.

✻

After five minutes we are becoming used to the character of the court. I've noticed his backhand is a little shaky. I win the toss and elect to serve. The 'marker' — the umpire — standing at the net post calls out, 'Play'. I raise my racket head to my face and make the traditional pre-match bow to the silent spectators, then turn to offer the same respectful salute to my opponent.

✻

THE FIRST BEAUTIFUL GAME

If you are a novice spectator, you are probably intrigued by the bizarre court and unfolding spectacle, and want to understand more before the match commences.

The most confusing aspect of tennis is its name. In England the sport is called 'real tennis', but it is known as 'court tennis' in the United States and 'royal tennis' in Australia. The French still call it 'jeu de paume' – game of the palm – even though tennis has been played with a racket, not the hand, for over five hundred years. It is commonly believed that the term 'real' derives from 'royal' and refers to the origins of the sport as a pastime for monarchs. This is an etymological myth. The appendage 'real' was only added to tennis in the 1870s to distinguish it from the new outdoor craze of 'lawn tennis'.[4] 'Real' means 'genuine' or 'original'.

How do you actually play? As in lawn tennis, a net divides the court in half, and you can play either singles or doubles. Points are generally scored in the familiar way – 15, 30, 40, deuce – and matches are the best of three or five six-game sets. But there the similarities end. Tennis is played on an enclosed court, a little larger than a lawn tennis court, with high black walls on all four sides. Along three of the walls are angled wooden roofs known as 'penthouses,' rising from a height of around six feet and resembling the sloping roofs of a cloister courtyard. The ball can both hit the walls, and roll and bounce along the penthouses.

The penthouses are visible in this photo of the court in Oxford, built in 1798. Along the left-hand wall below the penthouse are the 'galleries', large windows filled with netting. Hitting the ball into the 'winning gallery' (the most distant of these openings), which contains a small bell, is one way of winning the point. Points are also won by hitting two other targets: the 'grille', the square just visible in the back right-hand corner; and the 'dedans', a long netted window at the end of the court where spectators sit and from where the photo was taken. On the wall opposite the galleries there is an

The tennis court in Merton Street, Oxford.[5]

Plan of a typical tennis court.[6]

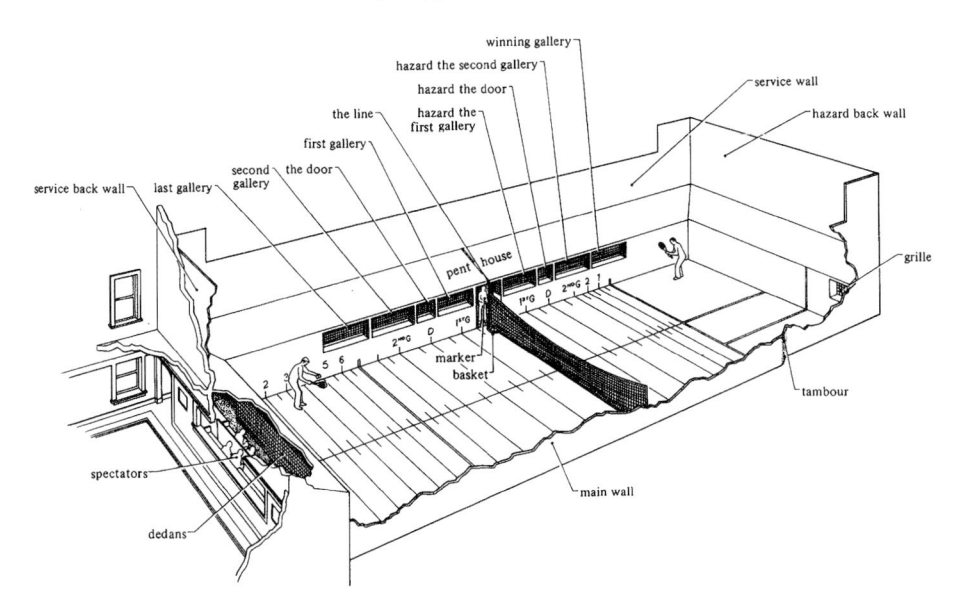

angled buttress jutting out — the 'tambour' — that, if struck, deflects the ball in unexpected directions. Playing tennis is like being inside a giant pinball machine, with the ball ricocheting off the walls and roofs, and striking targets.

The asymmetries of the court are echoed in the racket, whose head is angled to one side, making it easier to hit a low-bouncing ball. The balls are solid, containing a cork core wrapped in string and hand-sewn with a felt cover. Club professionals spend around a quarter of their time producing the balls with a technique unchanged over hundreds of years, in addition to stringing rackets, giving lessons and competing in tournaments.

That is enough of an introduction for the moment. The match is about to begin.

*

My opponent, a young Australian named Kieran Booth, skips around like a boxer, impatient for my opening serve. I take my time. I hit the ball underarm with plenty of spin. It traces a quiet curve through the air. Then it bounces once on the sloping penthouse roof and drops down into the back left-hand corner of the court. He steps forward and tries to volley the ball cross-court. An aggressive and risky shot. And the ball strikes the top of the net. I'm relieved: it's bad luck to lose the first point.

Each point I try a different serve. A railroad. A giraffe. Then a bobble. Kieran continues in aggressive mode. He smacks the ball as hard as possible, mostly without success. He hits it as if he hates it. But I also sense that his tactics mask nervousness. I win the first game easily: 15-love, 30-love, 40-love, game.

The second game is more complex. I'm still not used to the court's floor speed: the ball skids fast and low, hitting the wooden frame of my racket. His point. The court is larger than my home court in Oxford too. I respond by pushing the ball deeper and wider than usual. A few spectators murmur in appreciation at my accurate ball placement.

One more point and I'll have the game. I wipe my sweaty palm on my shorts and prepare to serve. 'Come on, this one,' I mutter to myself. I swing the racket in front of me in a pendulum motion and hit the ball with tremendous spin just above ankle height — an underarm twist. It flies upwards, then skips once, twice, three times on the penthouse. Kieran allows the ball to bounce on the floor. But he misjudges its spin and fails to move his feet. Hopelessly out of position, he lunges awkwardly at the ball and strikes the air with flailing racket. It's an embarrassing moment of Buster Keaton comedy that he will not repeat.

*

We live in a standardised world. Supermarkets provide us with apples of uniform colour and diameter. We buy a new jacket or sofa or car, hoping to stand out from the crowd, then notice a stranger with the same one. We deliberate over competing brands of washing powder then discover they are all owned by the same corporation.

Tennis defies the standard. Every court is slightly different in its dimensions and angles, its floor and wall speeds, the seams of its balls. Pick up a book on the game and you will learn, for instance, that the court at Hayling Island is around three foot longer and two foot wider than the Oxford court, and that the Oxford penthouse is over a foot narrower. Tennis courts are a celebration of uniqueness and diversity. They are individual characters — each with its personality and history, its peculiar tics and quirks. Each one should be approached differently for a successful conversation on court.

In lawn tennis everyone serves in roughly the same way and from the same position on the court, just behind the baseline. But in tennis you can serve from almost anywhere you wish. As a result tennis players have, over the centuries, developed dozens of distinct serves with different trajectories and spins. So just as there is no standard-sized court, there is no standard service. The names of the serves celebrate their character. The 'giraffe' has a long neck, flying high into the air. The 'railroad' is straight, hard and powerful. The 'boomerang' doubles back

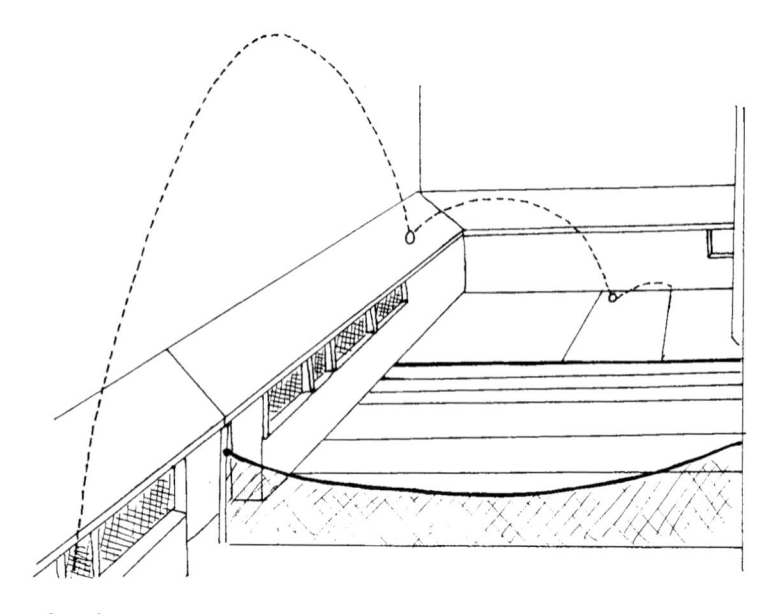

The path of a giraffe serve. The ball is hit in a high arc then bounces off the penthouse.[7]

on itself. The 'caterpillar' jumps along the penthouses, its arcs resembling multiple humps.

The service in lawn tennis resembles the conversational opener, 'How are you?' It is predictable, boring and rarely produces an unusual exchange. In contrast, the various services in tennis are like beginning a conversation with, 'In what ways would you like to be more creative?' or 'What are the limits to your compassion?' Tennis allows me to live in a world in which 'How are you?' is only one of many possibilities.

Anyone watching top professionals play lawn tennis will also notice how the serve is not only a tedious conversational opener but usually ends the discussion. On most surfaces apart from clay, the game is a spectacle of power serving and often little else. In tennis, however, it is almost impossible to serve an ace; the serve is more a way of putting the ball into play than winning the point. Because the serve does not dominate, the receiver is usually able to respond, so the first word of the point is seldom the last.

The great nineteenth century French player 'Biboche' (Charles Delahaye), contemplating serving a giraffe.[8]

When serving, a tennis player is generally attempting to limit the kind of return his or her opponent can make, such as by coaxing the serve to hug the side wall so closely that they can barely get their racket behind it and are forced to return down the line. Spin and accuracy are more important than speed. The strategic thinking required to choose the appropriate serve, combined with the skill needed to master the variety of service techniques and the sheer beauty of the different ways the ball arcs through space, transforms serving in tennis into an art form.

✽

Today I feel unusually confident. I return serve with a smooth and severe certainty. The ball drops quickly off the penthouse. I volley it cross-court. It curves away from Kieran as he stretches to reach it on his forehand. Another ball speeds dangerously fast towards my head. I swivel quickly and block it back into the base of the tambour. It's a moment of spontaneous creativity. The ball rolls along the floor, unreturnable.

He's four games to one down and tries some new serves. I adjust my feet in a rapid quickstep, hitting the next three returns straight past him into the dedans. Kieran is clearly frustrated. He utters some unintelligible oath. I sprint across for a backhand and hear the distinctive sharp twang from my racket of a ball struck with perfect timing.

I am no longer strategising: I move around the court swiftly, naturally, free, with little thought about how and where to hit the ball. The division between mind and body begins to dissolve.

I hit another volley, this time into the winning gallery. The bell attached to the netting rings in recognition. Applause. It's only half an hour into the match and the first set is over. Six games to one.

✻

From the age of seven, Helen Keller, who was both deaf and blind, communicated with the world through her hands. Beginning in 1887, her teacher, Annie Sullivan, would hold Helen's hand and use finger movements on her palm to translate what someone was saying. Helen often placed her other hand lightly on the person's face or lips as they spoke to decipher their words and feelings. She later wrote that a drawing of her mind would have to depict not her head but her hands, for this was the main place she experienced thought.[9]

While I instinctively locate my thinking self in my head, Helen Keller's experience is familiar. Sometimes when playing tennis I feel that I am 'in' my right hand. As the part of my body connected to the racket, it seems to control what the racket is doing, usually without explicit 'instruction' from my head. My hand is the centre of my being, even though I know that other parts of my body, like my forearms, are helping me hit the ball. By focusing hard I can also 'think myself into' my racket head.

THE WORDLESS CONVERSATION

If this sounds strange to you, try closing your eyes and repeatedly clenching and unclenching your fist. If you focus intently on this for a few moments, concentrating on the various parts of your hand moving through space, other bodily sensations and thoughts eventually fade away and you will begin to feel yourself to be 'in' your hand. This kind of sensation is understood by those who practise the Alexander Technique and is probably similar to the experience of football players who say, 'I think with my feet'. It makes the purported distinction between mind and body seem absurd.

When I feel overwhelmed by writing and thinking, tennis restores my sense of mind-body balance by helping to shake up my brain and to relieve it of cramp and knotted thoughts. A solution to some complex problem, such as how to restructure a story I am working on, often comes in an unexpected instant in the middle of tennis practice. This would not surprise neurophysiologists. Recent brain research shows how physical activities such as walking or yoga stimulate neural activity that can help with problem-solving, trigger fresh thoughts or bring back forgotten memories.[10] I hope that the asymmetries of the court and irregular bounce of the ball inspire me to think unusual and unconventional thoughts, and to take surprising angles on intellectual problems.

*

I begin the second set slowly, perhaps still shocked by my success in the first. I scrape through to win the first two games. My opponent then changes tactics: he does spinning serves that bounce short and awkwardly up into my body. The first one surprises me. My limbs entangle like a confused octopus. The ball rebounds off my racket frame and rolls into the net. As the next one comes, I stretch forward to volley the ball at knee height before it bounces. Again the net. He tries a third time. I let it bounce but over-hit the return. He slams the simple shot assertively into the grille.

I become anxious. What if he continues to trap me with this serve? How should I respond? Am I losing my concentration? The questions fill my head, an unwanted distraction from the game.

Kieran's confidence grows. He lunges for a backhand and guides it skilfully down the line over the high part of the net. I'm left waiting for the ball in the opposite corner.

I begin to flounder and panic. He gives me a straightforward shot. The words 'easy ball' fill my mind. And I drive it into the net. 'Roman!' I shout out in frustration. It's a rare outburst, a sign that I am unravelling. I'm four games to two down and see no prospect of winning the set. I lose a close deuce game. I look into the small crowd in the dedans. Even friendly faces do not meet my eye. I am alone.

✻

I have very few memories of my childhood before my mother died. I look back and see images of myself in the second-hand memories of family photos. In one of these fading snapshots, taken when I was nine, I am sitting on my father's lap, laughing. I'm wearing white sports gear, my skin is sweaty. Perhaps Dad had just driven me back from one of the junior lawn tennis tournaments I used to play in. I imagine that my mother, at the time dying from cancer, took the photo.

I recollect nothing of the service on the day of my mother's funeral, when I was ten. All I remember is that during the wake I asked my father if he would take me to a friend's place to play lawn tennis. He did, and so I spent the afternoon hitting a ball across a net.

I was recently back home in Sydney, over twenty years later, showing Kate the places of my childhood. As we walked along a suburban street one day, I suddenly saw my teenage self cycling past us on the way to lawn tennis practice, then disappearing left into a driveway up ahead. And I was gone before I had a chance to ask myself why I had left the wake.

✻

I'm thirty-love down. Kieran needs only two points for the second set. My racket grip feels slippery. A railroad service comes straight and hard along the penthouse edge. I risk a volley return. A great shot, he'll never reach it. But he does. His mis-hit stroke scrapes over the net and nicks the edge of the tambour. The spectators' delight deflates me. I lean against the wall, despondent. What the hell is going on here? My next return is pathetic, halfway down the net. The set is over, six games to two. One set all.

*

In Zen Buddhism, the purpose of meditative practice is to retain your 'shoshin' or 'beginner's mind'. The mind should be empty and at the same time ready for anything, open to all possibilities; you should have no thoughts of future achievement or longing. A related idea in a treatise on the Zen approach to archery is that technical knowledge is insufficient to become a master of an art; you must transcend technique so that the art becomes an 'artless art' emerging from the unconscious. Instead of aiming at the target, you should aim at yourself.[11]

While realising it has become a cliché to say so, I have been inspired by such aspects of Zen Buddhism. When practising, I often focus on watching the seam of the ball spinning towards me rather than thinking about taking my racket back early, or hitting the grille, or winning the point. Soon I am no longer trying to watch the ball; I am just watching it. Unlike other Zen acolytes, however, I am equally inspired by Pierre Etchebaster, tennis World Champion from the 1920s to the 1950s, who claimed that he always tried to count the stitches on a slow bouncing ball.[12]

✻

I must recover my beginner's mind. The first serve of the final set bobbles towards me on the penthouse. I concentrate intently on the ball. It hangs suspended at the top of its bounce. The world is on pause, silent. I pound the ball into the main wall and it rebounds into the dedans. My point.

This intense focus is not enough. I must also make strategic changes. I remember his weak backhand in the warm-up and realise I have failed to test it. So I start returning serve wide to his left. The first he hits back but not in the middle of the strings. The second lands close to the wall under the galleries. His swinging racket strikes the wall, not the ball. In the next point I play a shot short to his backhand. He stretches forward, loses balance, and misses. Our roles are reversing.

The games reach one-all. I'm stuck down the hazard end of the court. I desperately need a chase to get back to the service end. His next serve is overhit and rolls off the back penthouse. He probably expects me to blast it down the line into the dedans. Instead, I take the racket back feigning a hard shot, then slow down my swing and slip the ball just over the net with more spin than pace into the forehand corner. He moves the wrong way and the ball bounces twice, falling at 'chase one yard'.

✻

THE WORDLESS CONVERSATION

Early in Shakespeare's Henry V, King Harry informs the King of France that, through his great-grandfather Edward, he is entitled to 'some certain dukedoms' across the channel. In response the Dauphin, heir to the French throne, sends a mocking gift to Harry. 'What treasure, uncle?' asks Harry. The Duke of Exeter opens the box and replies, 'Tennis balls, my liege'. Harry turns to the French Ambassador, his initial sarcasm becoming fury:

> We are glad the Dauphin is so pleasant with us.
> His present and your pains we thank you for.
> When we have matched our rackets to these balls,
> We will in France, by God's grace, play a set
> Shall strike his father's crown into the hazard.
> Tell him he hath made a match with such a wrangler
> That all the courts of France will be disturbed
> With chases.

Using a tennis match to symbolise a forthcoming battle between England and France reflects the popularity of tennis in Elizabethan England. But only a tennis player can understand the full significance of Harry's words.

The net splits a tennis court into two sections, the service end and the hazard end. Players at the hazard end are at a disadvantage. Not only are they always receiving the serve and never serving themselves, they should also be ready for a ball that deflects sharply off the angled tambour and must prevent their opponent from hitting either of the two targets at the hazard end that win the point, the grille and the winning gallery. Thus when Harry threatens to strike the crown of the French King into the hazard, he is implying that France will be forced into a weak position, on the receiving end of Harry's wrath.

Harry continues his clever wordplay, telling the Ambassador 'that all the courts of France will be disturbed with chases'. Tennis players cherish the 'chase' although they dread explaining this confusing rule of the sport. The spirit of the chase most resembles the game of bowls or boule. The first player throws their ball, trying to get it close to a target, which is usually a very small ball. The aim of the second player is simply to throw their ball closer to the target, in order to win.

In tennis, a chase is usually created when the ball bounces twice on the floor at the service end. 'Chase one yard' means that the second bounce was on the line that is one yard from the back wall. When a chase occurs, the rally stops but no point is scored. The chase allows the player at the hazard end to swap sides of the court and occupy the more advantageous service end. After changing ends, this chase is 'played off': the receiving player must hit the ball so its second bounce is closer to the back wall than the one yard line. If they succeed they win the point; if not they lose it. As with boule, whoever is closest wins. Hitting the ball so the second bounce is in the narrow area between the one yard line and the back wall is extremely difficult. King Harry is saying that it is the English who will be laying chases against the French, rather than the other way around, and that England will thereby be placed in a stronger military position.

The chase is beautiful because is requires finesse. Tennis players are not only slamming the ball as hard as possible into the winning targets. They are also trying to stroke it smoothly to perfect length, out of their opponent's reach, so the second bounce is as close to the back wall as possible, laying an almost unbeatable chase and giving them entitlement to the service end of the court. In lawn tennis, by contrast, fine touch has almost disappeared. Subtle and elegant elements of the game, such as the drop shot or lob, are increasingly rare as brute strength becomes the norm.

✤

THE WORDLESS CONVERSATION

I've laid a chase so we swap ends. I walk towards the net post, as does Kieran. He respects the established ritual of allowing the player at the hazard end to pass around the net post first. As we brush past each other he hands me two balls. Another custom. He still looks fresh. I try to hide my heavy breathing.

*

The tradition of allowing the new server to come around the net post first is, for me, one of the most precious features of tennis. Whether the person at the hazard end is a pauper or a prince, a woman or a man, a stronger player or a weaker one, they are allowed to pass through first. Many social customs and ceremonies, such as the coronation of a monarch, or men holding doors open for women, symbolise or perpetuate authority. This one creates a moment of equality.

I do not mean to idealise the social relations of tennis. Until the 1970s, for instance, tennis was primarily a male pursuit. The author of a late Victorian book (*see overleaf*) on tennis mentions some famous female players but advises ladies to be spectators.[13] Although today there remain a few all-male clubs where such attitudes can be found, tennis is no longer considered too fatiguing or dangerous for women.

*

Now at the service end, I find new energy. A quick succession of points gives me a four-one lead. I can see the end of the match before me. Just two more games. Don't think about it. Keep focused. Play it point by point, I whisper to myself.

Kieran does not give up hope. He starts going for his shots with unexpected force. I miss two easy volleys in a row. A thought flashes through my head: I've lost my last three matches in the final set. The thought passes, but something changes. I now hit the ball tentatively, trying to avoid errors. I lose the service end and miss a simple return of serve. I hear a couple of spectators clap. How can they applaud an unforced error? I breathe deeply a few times and play on. Now he feels the pressure and makes some errors.

A BALL-GAME OF MODERN TIME

WE may not wish to encourage our wives and daughters to emulate Nausicaa, Margot, Mademoiselle Bunel, or Madame Masson, and to compete with us in an exercise fatiguing to all, and to them possibly dangerous, but we accord to them a hearty welcome when they honour the 'dedans' with their presence.

THE WORDLESS CONVERSATION

Furious with himself, he shouts out in anger. The audience in the dedans is hushed.

*

In the mid-eighteenth century Voltaire wrote: 'How shameful it is to think that for the first performances of *Mithridate* and *Tartuffe* there was no worthier accommodation than the Star Tennis Court with the audience standing in the pit and with the dandies sitting amongst the actors on-stage'.[14] During the seventeenth and eighteenth centuries, particularly in France, tennis courts were increasingly used as theatres. They were a favoured venue for the playwright and actor Molière (author of *Tartuffe*) and his troupe Théâtre Illustre, since only a few purpose-built theatres existed. Such arrangements also suited court owners, who realised that their dwindling revenue caused by the declining popularity of tennis could be compensated by temporarily renting their courts for dramatic performances.

Most sports, tennis included, can be their own drama. The athletes, like actors in a play, represent something beyond themselves: they embody a social struggle or a clash between ideologies or cultures.[15] A famous instance is the heavyweight boxing bout between the African-American Joe Louis, son of an Alabama sharecropper, and the German Max Schmeling, Aryan symbol of Nazi oppression. Held before 70,000 sweating spectators on June 22, 1938 at Yankee Stadium, New York City, the contest was a microcosm of racial politics and the approaching war. 'A right to the body, a left hook to the jaw, and Schmeling is down!' cried the commentator. He stayed down. The encounter lasted 124 seconds. In a country of lynchings, discrimination and segregation, Louis became an idol to Americans of all colours.

The crowd at this tennis match are not waiting for a knockout. They realise, however, that the game has reached its dramatic climax and the outcome is uncertain. They assess the character of each player. Roman is older, more experienced. He will probably remain calmer in these tense final moments and wear down his opponent with steady play. Kieran is less predictable but more talented. He could easily unleash a series of winning shots to take the match. This may not be democracy versus fascism or black against white. But the tennis players represent two distinct approaches to life: balance and composure versus spontaneity and inspiration.

✻

I'm now five-three up and leading forty-fifteen. Two match points. Experience and composure will triumph.

I serve and he pounds his return down the line. I dive across for a desperate backhand volley, both feet in the air. I can't reach it and the ball sneaks into the dedans. His point. My next serve is tight against the side wall. Kieran's return is too high and hits the back penthouse. Surely this is game over. The ball slowly rolls off. I watch it bounce . . . racket back, step in . . . my shot strikes the top of net cord . . . hovers a moment . . . then drops my side of the net. I close my eyes in despair. Deuce. There are mutterings from the crowd.

As if they know something.

Kieran takes the game. And the next one.

The score is five-all. Whoever wins the next game, wins the set and match.

✻

I am interested in the art of losing. Like anyone, I can enjoy victory, at least for a moment. But the joy soon fades and I feel increasingly uncomfortable, even embarrassed. I have a strange allergy to coming first, reaching the top, defeating adversaries, being a hero. The desire for such achievement seems to me an anxiety for social status emerging from our bad habit of judging ourselves through the eyes of others. This anxiety is manufactured by school exams, by parental pressures, by Hollywood films, by advertising. 'Be the best!' shout the army recruitment ads. What for? I prefer to judge myself against my own past performance or imagined potential, whether in tennis, work or other realms.

Most victors look down on the defeated; and they, in turn, live in the shadow of inadequacy. There is already enough personal insecurity in the world and I don't wish to add to it. Victory is the enemy of empathy.

*

The final game. Over two hours of struggle are now distilled into a few moments. It's his chance for a big win against a higher-ranked opponent. I desire dignity, at least. I no longer sense the spectators.

We both play nervously. There are loose shots. We can't put them away. He has a match point – but then double faults. Deuce. Kieran wins the next point: his advantage. Can I save the match? His serve comes towards me. It skims the penthouse dangerously. I'm too frightened to volley it. I let the ball bounce off the back wall. It sits up for me, waiting. And I strike it firmly. Straight into the net.

*

Perhaps tennis, as King Harry believed, is war by other means. But remove an undiluted desire for crushing victory and its metaphorical potential expands.

A good tennis player is a versatile conversationalist. Listen hard to understand your opponent's individual abilities, intentions, insecurities. Respond instinctively to the surprising angles and spins of each idiosyncratic court. Choose between a score of different serves to open the discussion and be ready to reply to all of them. Prolong the conversation with lengthy rallies when necessary. At times be assertive and uncompromising to hit the winning targets. Then change the pace with subtle shots to lay the perfect chase. While constantly switching between personalities, remember to talk with yourself.

The wordless conversation of a close tennis match is the model for an ideal dialogue, one-on-one, intense, intuitive, unexpected, creative. Whether you win or lose, the conversation has always changed you.

☆

We shake hands over the net. I force myself to look him in the eye. I thank the marker, who still stands attentively at the net post. 'Unlucky,' he consoles me. I gather up my rackets and towel, and return to the dressing room.

It's empty. I sit down, take off my shoes. My feet throb. I close my eyes. And the final shot appears before me — a simple return of serve driven into the net. 'You fool!' I hiss out loud. 'Two match points and a stupid shot to finish.'

I stand under the steaming shower and let the hot water wash off my sweat, my anger, my unwanted ambition.

2 From Abbots to Zealots

Why have people bandied balls back and forth over a drooping net for more than five hundred years? And why have they done it with such passion and obsession? Clues for answering these questions lie in the curious history of the game, which stretches from renaissance abbots to contemporary zealots.

ABBOTS

'Play is battle and battle is play,' wrote the cultural historian Johan Huizinga when discussing the close relationship between sports and games on the one hand, and warfare and violence on the other.[16] Many sports were originally conceived as training and preparation for war. The chivalric medieval tournament in Europe is amongst the most spectacular of examples. Activities such as jousting and the passage of arms converted the tournament into 'a theatre in which men competed with men, honing their fighting skills and implicitly preparing for the possibility of real battle'. In the final years of the tournament, more knights were killed in the games themselves than on the battlefield.[17]

Some historians believe tennis emerged from the tournament, especially the passage of arms, a stylised battle for a castle in which the participants attacked and defended a strategic bottleneck, such as a castle gate. Those who defended were known as 'ceux de dedans' or 'those on the inside'. This idea is retained in tennis, where players must attempt to prevent their opponents from hitting the ball into the winning opening called the dedans.[18]

But how exactly did this mock attack on a castle give birth

to tennis? The passage of arms is said to have inspired medieval football, a violent entertainment in which each team kicked and poked a leather pouch stuffed with hay through an opening defended by their opponents. This game then shifted into the more genteel surroundings of monastic cloisters – probably in northern France or Flanders – where the ball was propelled by the hand and could roll along the sloping arcade roofs, which became the model for penthouses, the slanting roofs on purpose-built tennis courts. The *craticula* – a window in monastic buildings though which laymen could communicate with the monks – is thought to be preserved in the grille in modern tennis courts, a square in the corner of the receiver's end which, when hit, awards the serving player a point.[19] The implication is that monks were the first masters of the game, although it was soon taken up by members of the nobility and, later, by commoners when tennis spread to the streets.

If the origins of tennis lie in the passage of arms, early tennis players were the inheritors of a medieval cultural legacy to engage in activities that imitated war-play. Today's tennis fanatics are, therefore, the modern incarnation of chivalric knights. They simply lack armour and horses, and use rackets instead of swords.

Even if the game did not originate in the cloister, there is little doubt that monks have appeared on tennis courts. According to one historian: 'A certain monk, while playing with the king [Louis XII] against two lords, made a brilliant stroke which decided the set in the king's favour, who then exclaimed, "Ah! that is the stroke of a monk!" "Sire," replied the monk, "whenever it may please you, it shall be the stroke of an abbot." An abbey happened to be vacant at that moment; and this the monk received, as a reward, both for his stroke and for his witty rejoinder.'[21]

Religious figures have been involved in tennis in other ways. In 1451 the Bishop of Exeter, Edmund Lacy, complained about tennis matches between clergy and laity in a local churchyard,

Medieval tennis players used their hand to hit the ball instead of a racket. This game appears to be taking place in a cloister courtyard.[21]

which resulted in 'heinous and blasphemous words' and 'squabbles, disputes, brawls and battles of words'. All this, he claimed, was distracting good Christians from saying their prayers.[22]

An alternative to the cloister theory is that tennis derived, more humbly, from medieval street games, such as those played in the north of Italy. Medieval shop fronts were frequently covered by a sloping roof to protect goods laid out for sale beneath them. This form of roof, known as a 'pentys' and later 'penthouse', projected out onto the street from the first floor for two or three feet. When ball games were played on the street it became common to serve the ball up onto these slanting roofs to begin the point. Tennis later shifted indoors and the roofs became the model for the angled penthouses that surround three of the walls on a tennis court; the server must hit the ball onto one of these penthouses to start each point. The Italian connection is that there are still a number of ancient Tuscan ball games played in village streets that have

The sloping roofs above medieval shopfronts are retained in a miniature roof used in a game of tennis being played by naked babes in seventeenth century France.[23]

rules similar to those in tennis (such as the chase), although the sloping roofs have now disappeared. However, the game of *pantalera*, played in Alba (near Turin), retains a small sloping roof onto which the ball must be served before it rolls into play.[24]

BARTHOLOMEW MASSACRE

Following its medieval origins, tennis became a new craze across Europe in the sixteenth and seventeenth centuries. The game was primarily played in France and England, but was also popular in Italy, Spain, Germany, and the Low Countries. But who exactly were the players? In France tennis was played by the nobility, including a succession of kings. Not even the horrific St Bartholomew massacre in Paris in 1572 could deter Henry IV from playing tennis: 'at a time when not only the lives of hundreds of his best friends and followers had been sacrificed, but his own head was in the most imminent jeopardy, he could not refrain from rising at daylight the next morning to continue a game of tennis'.[25]

Commoners also played in the hundreds of courts – both indoor and outdoor – that existed in every quarter of Paris, although there is little documentation of their experiences. The first professional players appeared around this time. Some were engaged as teachers for the king, while others ran their own courts and made balls and rackets. In 1610 the status of tennis professionals was such that they were raised by royal charter to the rank of a Corporation through the establishment of the *Communauté des Maîtres Paumiers-Raquetiers*. In effect this changed the status of tennis from a mere game to an art, like horsemanship or fencing.[26]

Tennis spread to England and, as in France, was favoured by the nobility and monarchs. It became known as both the 'king of games' and the 'game of kings'. Henry VIII was the most famous, and possibly the most skilled, amongst England's early royal players, enjoying the sport at Hampton Court Palace and other royal residences. Charles II may have been the least talented. As the diarist Samuel Pepys wrote in 1664: 'To the Tennis Court, and there saw the King play at tennis and others; but to see how the King's play was extolled, without any cause at all, was a loathsome sight.'[27] Certainly the game was also played by those outside the aristocracy. In 1558 a French ecclesiastic, visiting England, noted tennis being played by artisans such as hatters and joiners.[28]

The refinement of tennis may have made it particularly attractive in the sixteenth and seventeenth centuries when there was a growing desire amongst the European upper classes to desist from the vulgar violence of their medieval forebears and instead indulge in more sophisticated activities, such as music or art.[29] Tennis was one of the few available options for those nobles who wished to engage in a healthy physical activity that was nevertheless genteel; there was nothing particularly uncouth about striking a ball over a net and the

A member of the Guild of Rackets- and Brush-Makers, the corporation that preceded establishment of the Guild of Master-Professionals and Racket-Makers in 1610. Here the racket serves as a sporran.[30]

players needn't have any unsavoury physical contact with each other.[31] Most sports that we now consider 'refined' or 'gentlemanly', such as cricket, did not yet exist in a recognised form. Tennis was no doubt also played for reasons of prestige and social cachet.[32] Once the game became favoured by French and English kings in the sixteenth century, it was considered, like hunting, a fitting pursuit for members of the nobility.

Tennis went into decline in the eighteenth century. By 1767 there were only 12 Master Professionals in Paris and a decree of 1771 forbade the recruitment of new apprentices due to the lack of courts.[33] By the time that the tennis court in Versailles was used for a momentous meeting in the French Revolution, in 1789, tennis was already becoming an anachronism, both on the continent and in England. Some members of the nobility continued to shuffle around the courts but common city-

*German nobles bandying the ball about in the early seventeenth century.*³⁴

dwellers no longer played or wagered on the game, and most monarchs had lost interest. Courts were more likely to be used as theatres than for tennis. By the nineteenth century tennis was only played at a small number of locations in France and England, many of them private homes of the aristocracy, and at a few courts in the United States and Australia, where the game had spread due to English influence.

What explains the rapid decline of tennis? Historians have failed to provide any clear answers and I can only offer hypotheses: that new and more attractive arenas for gambling emerged; that commoners who previously aped their social superiors by playing tennis no longer thought the aristocracy deserved such reverence and imitation; that increasing urban property prices and taxes made the cost of building and running a court prohibitively expensive; that the rise of Puritanism after the Reformation helped give games like tennis a frivolous and even sinful reputation; that surviving the English civil war and Cromwell's rule in the seventeenth century was more important than playing tennis; that the game required too much physical exertion for 'civilised' gentlemen, who preferred less vigorous pastimes like cricket; and that it became overshadowed by team sports like football (soccer) which appealed to collective identities such as 'the nation' in an age of patriotism and empire. These may be some of the reasons why tennis had become a largely forgotten sport by the late nineteenth century, with the upper classes its custodians until the game's revival in the 1970s.

CONSTIPATION

The health benefits of tennis have been touted for centuries and contributed to the popularity of the game. In his *Description of the Chief Callings Useful to Society*, published in 1698, the German author Christoff Weigel argued that tennis was a fine cure for constipation suffered by slothful aristocrats: 'Water which stands without any movement finally transmutes into putrescence and begins to stink; and the human body without its required movement and motion shows a slow circulation of the blood resulting in constipation, whereby residual fluids turn putrid and pungent and thus cause illness and finally even lead to an early death. In order to forestall such worrisome evils, some amusing movements have been devised for such personages whose nobility and rank consist in all manner of stillness and but little motion. Of such exercises, the game at ball is one of the noblest and most pleasurable as well as the most useful . . . In special ballhouses found in part in the palaces of lords and in part in the larger towns, they play with a small ball and racket. It is useful for the gentle reader to know that this game not only gives pleasure, but also is, if moderately used, highly beneficial to the maintenance of one's health.'[35]

The first treatise on tennis by a professional player, Pierre Barcellon's *Rules and Principles of Tennis* (1800), begins with a categorical statement that 'of all exercises Tennis is the most agreeable and the most salutary for the health'. Although not explicitly concerned with constipation, Barcellon believed that the game warded off rheumatism and alleviated the harmful effects of wearing tight pants: 'A man going into the Tennis court is usually free of limb and unencumbered; all his members, no longer restricted by his everyday wear, allow the blood to circulate freely, his breathing is no longer hampered and his knees bend more easily. He becomes supple and light of foot, he acquires poise and his limbs, being stretched, develop in strength and vigour; health-giving sweat exudes copiously, his muscles increase their elasticity and from the very depths of his enjoyment he is imbued with grace and good health.'[36] What higher recommendation could a sport ask for?

DEATH

While tennis clearly has health benefits, it seems to be amongst the world's more dangerous sports:

- In 1316, Louis X ('the quarrelsome') was unusually hot after playing tennis in the forest of Vincennes. He retired to a cool grotto where he caught a chill, and died soon afterwards as a result.[37]

- In 1498, at the Château of Amboise, Charles VIII banged his head on a door lintel on his way to watching a tennis match. Although apparently unharmed, it was not long before he toppled over backwards, dead.[38]

- In 1548 in Augsburg, Germany, a brand new tennis court suddenly collapsed, killing three people. The town council immediately ordered the builder to reconstruct the court at his own expense.[39]

- In his *Essays*, which first appeared in 1580, Montaigne writes of his brother's death: 'Captain Saint-Martin, twenty-three years old who had already given pretty good proof of his valour, while playing tennis was struck by a ball a little above the right ear, with no sign of contusion or wound. He did not sit down or rest, but five or six hours later he died of an apoplexy that this blow gave him.'[40]

☠ Even more quarrelsome than Louis X was the painter Caravaggio, who fled Rome in 1606 after killing Ranuccio Tomassoni following an argument over a game of tennis.[41]

☠ In Dublin in 1609, hot-tempered aristocrat Lord Howth entered a tennis court with a band of men intending to punish Sir Roger Jones, who had accused him of being a coward. A swordfight ensued on court, with one man being killed and others injured.[42]

☠ A record from 1612 describes the following case of tennis suicide: 'A son of the Bishop of Bristol, his eldest, of nineteen or twenty years old, killed himself with a knife, to avoid the disgrace of breeching which his mother, or mother-in-law (I know not which) would need have put him to, for losing his money at Tennis.'[43]

☠ Around 1630 a boy named Jean le Camus, who later became a well-known tennis professional in Paris, narrowly escaped death from a lion which was exhibited on a stage in a tennis court.[44]

☠ In 1751 the Prince of Wales mysteriously dropped dead. According to physicians, the cause was a blow from a tennis ball in his stomach three years earlier, which had broken open an abscess.[45]

Tiepolo's The Death of Hyacinth, *with a detail of the racket in the bottom right-hand corner.*[46]

The obvious conclusion to draw is that any attempt to eradicate monarchy is not best achieved by revolution or political reform, but by encouraging the monarchs to play a little tennis. The hopes for a republic in the United Kingdom are limited by the fact that only one royal personage, Prince Edward, is a regular tennis player.

Tennis is dangerous not only for monarchs but for gods. In Greek mythology, Apollo accidentally killed Hyacinth by throwing a discus that struck him in the head. In 1752 the Venetian painter Tiepolo modified the story, so that Hyacinth

Enormous pantaloons were fashionable in the renaissance (left) *while soft caps became favoured in the eighteenth century* (right).⁴⁷

was knocked out and killed by a stray ball while Apollo was teaching the beautiful young man how to play tennis. A close-up reveals the excellent stringing on Hyacinth's racket.

ENORMOUS PANTALOONS

The tennis court has long been a favoured arena to display one's good fashion sense. During the renaissance enormous pantaloons were popular. While it would seem impossible to run swiftly in such awkward clothing, it should be noted that early tennis matches often had three people on each team, so the players probably didn't have to move around too much. In the eighteenth century, tennis clothing was more streamlined and elegant, with players wearing neat knee-length trousers,

42

The conservative attire of nineteenth century English gent The Honourable Alfred Lyttleton (above left) hardly compares to the stylish outfit of French professional Edmund Barre (above right).

Elbows and knees appear in contemporary tennis clothing, modelled here by current World Champion Rob Fahey.[48]

with special soft tennis slippers and a soft cloth cap. In Paris the Master of the Court could supply you with a cap, trousers, shorts, pullover, stockings and shoes for a total of fifteen *sous*, although if you only wanted the cap the cost was two *sous*. In a book on tennis published in 1783 De Manevieux warns that clothes from a court can be damp and smelly because 'the servant often only gives them a very hasty wash,' and in her haste 'folds them up half dry'.[48] By the nineteenth century ankle-length trousers and a white long-sleeved shirt were the norm, although there were some opportunities for personal flamboyance. While the English amateur The Hon. Alfred Lyttelton wore resplendent whites, the French professional Edmund Barre added a cravat and decorative waist band to match his two-tone shoes. Since the 1970s the standard attire has been more utilitarian and is similar to what used to be worn by lawn tennis players before they fell for multi-coloured brand gear: white shorts and shirt for men, and a white skirt or shorts and shirt for women.

GAMBLING

Tennis courts have not only been the site of sporting activity, but also a favoured location for gambling, drinking, prostitution and other vices. Kings, queens and aristocrats across Europe have won and lost huge sums betting on the game:

☞ In January 1472, renaissance playboy and layabout Galeazzo Maria Sforza, Duke of Milan and son of a skulduggerous mercenary made famous in Machiavelli's *The Prince*, won 30 ducats of gold from his brother, Ludovico, gambling on tennis. The Duke also once lost eight ducats playing against his court trumpeter. He usually travelled with a personal team of professional players. According to his biographer, Galeazzo's great passions were sex, tennis (giocho de la Palla) and music: *'a venere &*

soza libidine / gran piacere se pigliava nel giocho de la Palla / e similamente faceva de la Musici.⁵⁰

☞ Henry VIII may have been the most extravagant — and least successful — tennis gambler in history. In a single day in October 1532 he lost around 50 pounds, which was about a thousand times more than what most people of his era earned in a week. But he didn't stop there: he went on to lose more than twice that amount playing dice on the same day. Over a three-year period Henry's betting losses in tennis, dice, cards and other games reached almost 3,250 pounds.⁵¹

☞ Anne Boleyn was busy betting on a chase while watching a tennis match in Greenwich when she was arrested by Henry VIII's men. She was not permitted to find out the results of her wager.⁵²

☞ Gambling swindles were often orchestrated by unscrupulous court markers who rigged the scoring. The problem became so acute in France that in the early seventeenth century, the guild of tennis professionals obliged all markers, before they could perform their function, to pass through an apprenticeship stage. The swindling, however, continued.⁵³

☞ Eighteenth century England was also prone to gambling scams at the tennis court. According to one account from 1775: 'So various are the deceptions of this game, that it is almost impossible for a stranger to go into a tennis-court, and bett without losing his money — so prostituted is this noble game to what it used to be, that instead of seeing only persons of first rank in England, as formerly, we see the Dedans now thronged with some of the most notorious sharpers in London.'⁵⁴

Gambling on tennis had far-reaching implications for renaissance thought. In 1494 the Italian mathematician Luca Paccioli published his *Summa de arithmetica, geometrica et proportionalita*, which set out the basic principles of algebra. Paccioli was also effectively the inventor of statistics, with his book containing an example concerning the probabilities surrounding the division of stakes in an unfinished game of tennis. This became known as 'the problem of the points' and was widely quoted in mathematical treatises in the sixteenth and seventeenth centuries.[55]

Demonstrating remarkable hypocrisy, the very same aristocrats who delighted in betting on the game sought to ban tennis amongst 'commoners', believing that it encouraged immoral and riotous behaviour. In 1388 in England, just after the Black Death, an Act of Parliament stated that servants and labourers were to 'leave all playing at Tennis or Football, and other Games called Coits, Dice, Casting the Stone, Kailes and other such importune Games'.

Ruling elites also believed that tennis distracted the people from more useful activities such as war. An Act of 1477 prohibited tennis and other games in favour of archery, a martial activity considered beneficial for the defence of the realm. The penalties for playing and betting on the game were severe: up to two years imprisonment and a ten pound fine. In 1541 Henry VIII, a very keen player and gambler on tennis, also decreed that tennis was an 'unlawful' game and that able-bodied men should busy themselves with bows and arrows. Such bans on tennis in favour of archery continued until the eighteenth century, long after archery ceased to have any military significance.[56] It seems that the laws prohibiting tennis were often ineffective or not enforced, as was also the case in France.

While tennis had to compete with other forms of gambling – including cockfighting, bear-baiting, dice and cards – it may have been peculiarly appealing because of the handicap system, which permitted opposing players to compete on a roughly equal basis even if they were of different standards.[57] This increased the tensions and risks, which are part of the gambler's search for excitement and uncertainty, while at the same time appealing to an archaic human trait: the belief in luck or fortune.[58] The development of alternative arenas for gambling in the eighteenth century, such as prize fighting and horse racing, may help account for the declining popularity of tennis during this period.[59]

HANDICAPS

In *Rules and Principles of Tennis* (1800), the French professional Pierre Barcellon wrote: 'Since the ability of players at Tennis varies infinitely, a system of handicapping has been devised by which the most skilled and the least skilled can be brought close to one another, without which it would be impossible for a weak player to compete with a very strong one.'[60] He then gave the example of the weaker player starting 30-love ahead of his opponent in each game. Tennis players have sometimes invented more eccentric handicaps to introduce an element of equality into their matches:

- The French professional Raymond Masson, owner of two tennis courts in Paris and World Champion in 1765, once played a match with the handicap of having to jump into and out of a barrel after each of his strokes while his opponent returned the ball.[61]

- In the nineteenth century the French champion Edmund Barre played a handicap match with the marker sitting on his shoulders. This handicap had a fictional precedent: in 1582 the German writer Fischart, in an adaptation of Rabelais's *Gargantua and Pantagruel*, had the wrestler Milo of Croton, a famous Olympic champion of Greek antiquity, play tennis with a live ox on his shoulders. Another of Barre's handicaps was to walk 43 miles to the court before the match, then play without his shots being permitted to hit any walls. He defeated his aristocratic opponent easily.[60]

☞ Charles 'Biboche' Delahaye, the star pupil of Barre, played a handicap match fully equipped in the uniform of the National Guard in heavy marching order, with knapsack, musket, shako and cross-belts. The outcome of the match is unknown.[63]

☞ In Brighton in 1844, the great amateur player Charles Taylor played a best of five sets match against a Mr. B. Smith while seated on a pony. Although the pony, shod with special leather shoes, is reported to have 'behaved remarkably well throughout the contest', Mr Taylor lost three sets to one.[64]

Contemporary tennis retains the handicap system discussed by Barcellon, although in a slightly more refined form. As in golf, each player has a 'handicap', which is a number denoting their skill. A very weak player may have a handicap of -60, with a good club player having a handicap of -20. The world's best players have handicaps approaching zero, and some have broken the zero barrier: the handicap of the current World Champion is around +16. If two players have a match 'off handicap', the difference between their handicaps is calculated and this translates into specific advantages for the weaker player and restrictions on the stronger player during the match. For example, if the handicap difference is six, the weaker player begins 15-love ahead in each game, thus only requiring three points to win a game compared to their opponent needing four points. For large handicap differences of over twenty, the stronger player may begin each game at minus 30 (thus requiring six points to win a game), will only be allowed one serve instead of the usual two, and may be banned from hitting winning targets such as the grille. My favourite handicap is the *bisque*, which allows the weaker player to claim one free point at any stage they wish during the set. Match results are fed into a computer programme that adjusts each player's handicap down or up, depending on whether they 'over-performed' or 'under-performed' given the handicap difference between the players.

This system works incredibly well and makes tennis one of the most egalitarian sports in the world. It is ironic, and perhaps surprising, that a game associated traditionally with the upper classes and snobbery contains such a strong element of equality. Although the World Championship is played 'off scratch', meaning no handicaps are involved, there are still major tournaments where the handicap system is used. Just imagine if Wimbledon were played with the lower ranked player beginning each game 15-love ahead and being allowed to hit the ball into the tram lines.

INVENTIONS

The most significant invention to have been based on tennis is the modern game of lawn tennis. On March 7, 1874, a tiny but significant article appeared in the London *Court Journal*. It read: 'We hear of a new and interesting game coming out, which is likely to attract public notice, now blasé with croquet and on the *qui cire* for novelty. It has been patented under the name of 'Sphairistike or lawn tennis'. It has been tested in several country houses, and has been found full of healthy excitement, besides being capable of much scientific play. The game is in a box not much larger than a double gun case, and contains, besides bats and balls, a portable court, which can be erected on any ordinary lawn, and is ornamental as well as useful'. The inventor was Major Walter Clopton Wingfield, who in the previous month had obtained a provisional patent on a 'New and Improved Court for Playing the Ancient Game of Tennis'.[65]

Wingfield's genius was to simplify the traditional game at a time when the growing middle class was desperate for anything new. He changed the rules, eliminating the chase and winning targets such as the grille or dedans, and allowing players to serve from either end of the court. Lawn tennis was also cheap as it did not require building a costly indoor court. His only failure was that the obscure term 'Sphairistike' – the name of a ball game played in ancient Greece – never caught on.

In its early years, the new game was considered far inferior to the original. In 1903 The Honourable A. Lyttelton wrote 'The Relation of Tennis to Other Games', which illustrates the Victorian obsession with Darwinism: 'The relation of any one particular game to other games has been but little considered, and few games present more opportunities for such consideration than Tennis. With lawn-tennis, indeed, the relation of Tennis is literally parental, though the ordinary laws of evolution here sustain a singular reversal. In the world of nature we are accustomed to observe the development of the rude into the highly finished, of the primitive into the complex, of the inferior into the superior. Here, however, the process is changed. The inferior has been the successor of the superior, and the offspring is cast in far more primitive form than the sire. Dedans and gallery, tambour and grille, have been lost in the struggle for existence; hazard-side and chase are deemed not the fittest to survive.'[66]

Both games had to compete with the development of team sports such as football (soccer), which were gaining mass popularity. From the late nineteenth century, when football shifted from being an elite sport to one played by Britain's new urban working class, local and national teams became representative symbols of working communities, cities and whole countries. Similarly, for early twentieth century cricketers in the West Indies, defeating England in a test match was part of the national struggle against racism and for independence from colonial oppressors.[67] Lawn tennis and tennis, in contrast, had little of this collective appeal or significance. Yet lawn tennis may have become so popular from the late nineteenth century precisely because it was not a team sport (except in doubles). The game reflected and reinforced the individualism of middle class Victorian England that was itself part of the larger individualist ideology of capitalism as it developed from the eighteenth century. On the lawn tennis court you would not be absorbed into the mass as you would be on a football pitch. The survival of tennis into the twenty-first century should also be partly understood as a product of this bourgeois individualism. Although there are competitions between teams, clubs and nations in tennis, the very structure of the sport, with individuals playing against each other, echoes the capitalist focus on self-interest.

JEREMY IRONS

Some people have their first encounter with tennis through the film adaptation of John Fowles's novel, *The French Lieutenant's Woman*, released in the early 1980s. At one point in the film Victorian gentleman scientist Charles Smithson (played by Jeremy Irons) travels from Lyme Regis to London, where he plays a game of tennis with his lawyer, Harry. Tennis boffins will recognise that they are at Queen's Club and that the marker (umpire) is the normally clean-shaven club Head Professional David Johnson, who looks bemused by the giant ginger mutton chops stuck on his face. The two gents thwack the ball around energetically in their long trousers. We see Charles do a weak serve that rolls around the penthouse. He then successfully defends a chase of three yards, hitting a difficult overhead to win the first set six games to five. It appears authentic. But look closely and you will realise the

Jeremy Irons as Charles Smithson in The French Lieutenant's Woman.[68] *Tennis players will recognise that his positioning on the court displays an acute lack of understanding of the general direction in which a ball should be hit.*

deception. The ball is so bouncy that they must be using conventional lawn tennis balls, which bounce twice the height of genuine tennis balls.

The scene shifts to the changing rooms where Harry remarks that his friend was playing 'sharp as a razor' and jokingly inquires whether it was due to the fine country grub he has been eating. 'It's good to hit a ball,' replies Charles, his face and voice impassive. And Harry retorts, 'You were hitting it as though you hated it'. The tennis court was one of the few places where a Victorian male could show his emotions.

The importance of sport as an arena for human beings – especially men – to express anger and other strong feelings has been a popular subject with psychologists.[69] One theory is that society itself creates pressures, anxieties and antipathies towards other people that require an outlet, and that sport therefore functions as one of the 'countermeasures against stress-tensions that [most human societies] themselves generate'.[70] Particularly violent sports like boxing may allow poorer participants to express anger at their sense of being rejected by an unjust society, of being outsiders, and provide opportunities for a kind of revenge.[71] Similarly, according to one anthropologist, Samoan sports such as club fighting were a means of venting 'excessive emotions connected with the life crises of birth, marriage and death'.[72] A second theory is that people favour aggressive sports because humans are naturally competitive. As a species we have always competed for food, mates and dominance. Sport is simply a manifestation and extension of the struggle for survival.[73] From this biological perspective, sport has been defined as a ritualised competitive struggle between members of the human species that does not result in slaughter.[74] Although tennis does not permit the violence and aggression of sports like boxing, rugby union and wrestling, it does allow for controlled expression of anger. And that may be why Charles Smithson, unhappy in love, was so glad to spend some time on the tennis court.

LADIES

Tennis was almost exclusively a male pastime until the 1970s. The few female players in the game's history are generally depicted as oddities and eccentrics. Margot, a young woman from Flanders, first appeared on the tennis courts of Paris in 1427. Referred to as the 'Joan of Arc of Tennis', she defeated most of the best male players with her powerful and cunning forehands and backhands.[75] In the mid-eighteenth century a Madam Masson, who kept the court in the Rue Grenelle St. Honoré, Paris, was known for her 'vigorous wrist' and ability to 'cut the ball well and to volley it readily'. But according to an historian of her day, she was also 'blest with a captious, jealous, and morose temper, which prompted her to quarrel about every stroke, when playing a hard game, while the marker was afraid to give an opinion unfavourable to her for fear of receiving a ball or two upon his body, and a poor dinner afterwards'.[76]

Women, if permitted into the precincts of a tennis court at all, were generally confined to the role of spectators, watching from the viewing area at the end of the court behind the dedans netting. They were certainly not expected to have the mental capacity to comprehend the game's complex rules. This is obvious from a treatise on the game by former British amateur champion J. M. Heathcote, published in 1903, in which he lampoons women for their inability to recognise the grille and their confusion of 'discs' with the bisque, the special bonus point that can be claimed by a player in handicap matches: 'Some ladies, indeed, have shown that the difficulty of understanding Tennis is not insuperable; some are thoroughly appreciative of a good stroke, and keenly enjoy a well-contested match. But the following are examples of some strange solecisms I have heard. A lady once asked me what was kept in the *yellow cupboard*, in the opposite corner of the court. Another asked, 'What are *discs*, and how do you take them?' tempting me to reply 'cum grano' or 'two at bed-time.' Another lady, who for the first time visited the 'dedans' at Lord's, after watching the play for some time, naïvely remarked to her companion, 'Why, they mark at this game just as they do at *tennis!*'[77]

The increase in women players in England from around the mid-1970s caused panic amongst some of the old school traditionalists, most of whom were former public schoolboys who had spent years isolated from female company in the City, the army, and in their all-male clubs. Their usual argument was that women's wrists are simply too weak to handle the heavy racket and ball. Players such as Lesley Ronaldson, Judy Clarke and Sally Jones proved them wrong.

Despite the evidence that tennis was a game suitable for both sexes, there remained stalwarts, particularly within the sport's governing body, the Tennis & Rackets Association

(T&RA), who did little to encourage women players and tournaments. Former men's World Champion, Chris Ronaldson, wrote an article under a pseudonym parodying the old school traditionalists, which was to appear in *Tennis* magazine in 1990. The editors withdrew the article at the last moment, fearing the furore it might create. Some years later his wife, Lesley Ronaldson – one of the founders of the Ladies Real Tennis Association (LRTA) in 1981 and a former British Ladies Open Singles Champion – read out the article at a T&RA annual dinner:

> Real tennis is a game *historically* unsuitable for women. Across a thousand years the sport has been played, watched, wagered on and written about by men, despite the fact that lesser activities have, almost from the outset, encouraged the participation of both sexes. Only in the last fifteen years or so have the great stone walls echoed to voices of a higher pitch, an indignity forced upon them by the present phase of feminism.
>
> Real tennis is a game *physiologically* unsuitable for women. Female wrists are too frail to wield the heavy racquets correctly, while female legs are too short and too slow to cover the large court adequately. The success achieved by those at the forefront of the women's game is a relative success only, one which has to be measured against the general incompetence. For the moment, mediocrity rules and so it will remain unless, as at Wimbledon, it becomes a game dominated by girls with chromosome irregularities that do nothing for the image of the fairer sex.
>
> Real tennis is a game *intellectually* unsuitable for women. The strategies have oft been compared with chess, and the theories are based upon the ball's changing axes of rotation and the judicious use of angles. It is well documented that female brains are decidedly inferior in terms of mathematical and spatial problems and, in simple terms, there are no

effective female players of chess or snooker. How, then, can they hope to perform well at a sport that requires these skills in abundance?

Real tennis is therefore a game *wholly* unsuitable for women. Future generations of players will scorn our feebleness in resisting the breakdown of traditional values and salute those few who have stood firm against this unnecessary encroachment into male territory. Suffer not these stalwarts to be apologetic in the defence of their principles; rather let them be proud of their duty to swim against the tide when it begins to ebb as, perforce, it will on occasion.

As for the women, let them play badminton.

Those sharing such views have almost disappeared from the game. A few lurk in the most traditional clubs, such as the Leamington Tennis Court Club, the only one in England that retains an all-male membership policy. According to a history of the club, written by one of its members: 'Leamington is a gentlemen's club and all gentlemen's clubs in the past existed in response to man's desire to get better acquainted with man, but not necessarily all men and certainly not women.' Amongst his excuses for the men only policy is that 'drinking to the point of intoxication on occasion, gambling and raffish behaviour are part of the tradition of most gentlemen's clubs and are generally not the sort of thing of which women approve.'[78] Most of the club members who support the all-male policy would be easily defeated by the current women's World Champion, Charlotte Cornwallis. Perhaps they should take up badminton.

MAYAS

Nobody took ball sports more seriously than the Aztecs and Mayas in pre-Colombian Mesoamerica (what is today Mexico and Central America). Archaeologists have discovered the remains of over 1,500 ballcourts and thousands of carved reliefs, statues and other artefacts that demonstrate the centrality of the 'ballgame' to Mesoamerican culture – although the exact rules for playing remain unclear. The ballgame was not just a frivolous pastime but a ritualistic practice that was a metaphor for life and death. The Aztecs revered Xolotl, their patron deity of the ballgame. In the Popul Vuh, the Mayan book of creation, the Hero Twins Hunahpu and Xbalanque are brilliant players who defeat the Lords of the Underworld in a ballgame contest.

The ballgame is far older than tennis and developed independently of it. Yet there are striking similarities between the two games. A fresco painted by Diego Rivera in the National Palace in Mexico City depicts a typical Aztec ballcourt encountered by the Spanish conquistadors in the early sixteenth century (*see overleaf*). The sloping walls or 'aprons' on either side of the ballcourt strikingly resemble the angled penthouses on a tennis court. The stone ring – which began to appear on Aztec ballcourts from around 1000 AD – is similar to the 'lune', a circular hole found high on the wall at either end of early tennis courts; in both sports, points were scored when the ball passed through the hole.

There are further shared features. Like tennis, the floor was usually made of stone and the ballgame could be played as singles or doubles, although the Mesoamericans might have up to eleven players on each team. Substantial wagers were also often made on the ballgame.[79]

Of course, there are some differences. The Aztecs and Mayas played with a rubber ball, unlike the cork and cloth ball used in tennis. While the Mesoamericans occasionally used bats, the ball was usually hit with the upper arms, thighs, hips and buttocks. There was frequently music to accompany the games, and the players would enhance their performance and experience with hallucinogenic substances such as the leaves of the datura plant and water lily rhizomes. A final difference concerns post-match etiquette. In the Mesoamerican ballgame, a

The pre-Colombian Aztec ballcourt by Diego Rivera alongside a German tennis court in Tübingen around 1600 (facing page).[80]

losing player might be ritually sacrificed, with the victor decapitating his opponent or cutting his heart from his chest.[81] In tennis, the winner will usually buy his or her opponent a drink.

Despite the differences, the commonalities suggest that the origins of tennis should not only be sought in medieval European history. There may be a tendency for all human civilizations to develop forms of adversarial ball play that serve some deep psychological need or social function.

NATIVE AMERICANS

North American indigenous tribes, such as the Yokut, Cherokee, Cheyenne, Mohawk and Choctaw, regularly played a game known to nineteenth century ethnographers as 'racket', which had some resemblance to tennis. The racket itself was a stick, curved at one end with strings woven across it like a tennis racket. Players divided into teams and used the rackets to carry and propel the ball through goals at either end of a long field. Like the ballgame of the Mayas and Aztecs, such ball sports were often imbued with religious and ritual significance.

'Racket' is believed to be the origin of the modern sport of lacrosse.[82] However, early observers thought the game was similar to tennis. According to an account of the Huron Indians in Ontario, written by Baron La Hontan in 1703: 'They have a third ball play not unlike our tennis, but the balls are very large, and the rackets resemble ours, save that the handle is at least three feet long. The savages, who commonly play at it in large companies of three or four hundred at a time, fix two sticks at 500 or 600 paces distant from each other. They divide into two equal parties, and toss up the ball half-way between the two sticks. Each party endeavours to toss the ball to their side; some run to the ball, and the rest keep at a little distance on both sides to assist on all quarters. In fine, this game is so violent that they tear their skins and break their legs very often in striving to raise the ball. All these games are made only for feasts or other trifling entertainments; for 'tis to be observed that as they hate money, so they never put it in the balance.'[83] Obviously the good baron believed it was more civilised to gamble recklessly on a sport than to approach it as a matter of ritual significance. He seems to have conveniently forgotten the less-than-civilised gambling swindles that were taking place on Europe's tennis courts as he wrote these lines.

POETRY

The popularity of tennis between the sixteenth and eighteenth centuries is reflected in it becoming a favourite allegorical subject for playwrights and poets. The sporting contest between two people was a convenient metaphor for love, war and moral struggles. In 'On a Tennis-court', a poem by Francis Quarles published in 1632, the court is transformed into the universe in which God and Satan battle for the human soul:

> *Man is a* Tenniscourt: *His Flesh, the Wall:*
> *The Gamster's God, and Sathan: Th' heart's the Ball:*

> The higher and the lower *Hazzards* are
> Too bold *Presumption*, and too base *Despaire*:
> The *Rackets*, which our restlesse *Balls* make flye.
> *Adversity*, and sweet *Prosperity*:
> The Angels keepe the *Court*, and marke the place,
> Where the *Ball* fals, and chaulks out ev'ry *Chace*:
> The *Line's* a Civill life, we often crosse,
> Ore which, the *Ball* not flying, makes a *Losse*:
> *Detractors* are like *Standers-by*, that bett
> With Charitable me: Our *Life's* the Sett:
> Lord, in this *Conflict*, in these fierce *Assaults*,
> Laborious *Sathan* makes a world of *Faults*;
> *Forgive them Lord, although he nere implore*
> For favour: They'll be set upon our score:
> O, take the *Ball*, before it come to th' ground,
> For this base *Court* has many a false *Rebound*:
> Strike, and strike hard, but strike above the *Line*:
> Strike where thou please, so as the *Sett* be thine.[84]

A decade earlier Théophile de Viau published a rather more risqué poem, which showed how seventeenth century players were awarded forty-five rather than forty-points for their manly triumphs:

> If you kiss her, count fifteen,
> If you touch the buds, thirty,
> If you capture the hill,
> Forty-five comes up.
> But if you enter the breach
> With what the lady needs,
> Remember well what I sing to you,
> You will win the game outright.

For these and other shocking lines the poet was put on trial and banished from Paris.[85]

The Tennis Court Oath by Jacques-Louis David. The angled tambour on the right-hand wall and the penthouses are clearly visible. The detail shows the basket, racket and balls in the bottom left-hand corner.[86]

REVOLUTION

Tennis is a game of tradition, so it is ironic that one of the most famous moments of the French Revolution occurred on a tennis court. In September 1789 the Deputies of the Third

Estate – the national assembly of common citizens – found their meeting hall in the palace of Versailles unexpectedly closed. Suspecting that this may be the first step in their formal dissolution, they sought an alternative venue. One Deputy, Dr Guillotin (inventor of a famous device for decapitation), remembered a tennis court owned by a friend on the rue du Vieux Versailles, so the 600 representatives trooped through the rain to occupy the nearby court. There, in defiance of the monarch, they swore a solemn oath 'to go on meeting wherever circumstances may dictate, until the constitution of the realm is established and consolidated on firm foundations'. The moment is immortalised in an unfinished drawing by Jacques-Louis David, *The Tennis Court Oath* (1791). The Deputies are crowded onto the court and filled with the fervour of liberty. Robespierre has his hands placed on his chest in an expression of impassioned sincerity and virtue. The People look on in hope from the side galleries and from the windows above as the billowing drapery signals the winds of change blowing through France.[87]

Tennis players, however, will notice features of the court such as the angled tambour sticking out from the right hand wall and the pitched roofs of the penthouses. In the bottom left corner they will spot familiar objects: a tennis racket, a woven wicker basket for the balls, and three balls, ignored by the Deputies, lying on the floor.

SEWING

Tennis professionals are amongst the few men in our society who are adept at sewing. All tennis balls are made by hand and the final part of the process involves the professional stitching on a felt cover. This procedure has barely changed since the eighteenth century. The average assistant professional spends around nine hours a week making tennis balls. Such a large amount of time is required because each court needs a stock of

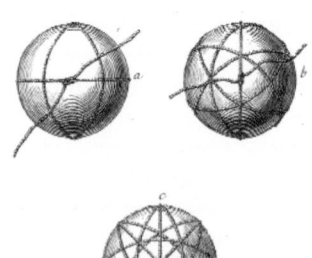

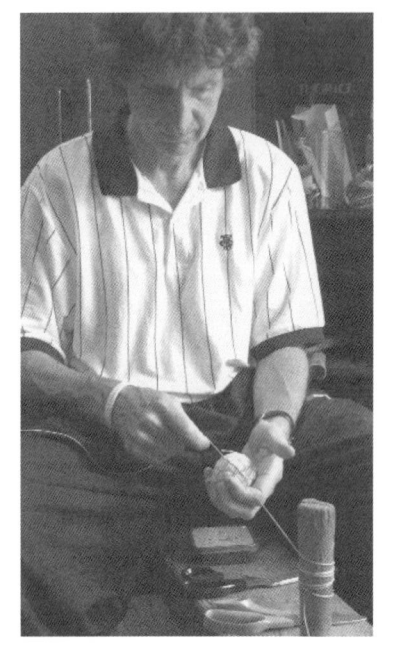

Ball-making in eighteenth century France (above).

Ball-making in twenty-first century England (left and below). The methods have hardly changed in three hundred years. The balls continue to be hand-sewn and tied in the same pattern.[88]

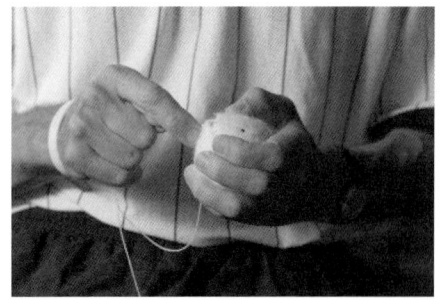

hundreds of balls: there are usually 70 balls on court at any one time and these must be re-covered after a few weeks of play.

The following extract from a 1999 technical study on how a tennis ball is made gives some sense of the painstaking work tennis professionals have carried out for hundreds of years on behalf of amateur players:

64

Step 1: Cutting the Cork
Four wine corks are chopped up with a knife, each into 16 pieces by cutting along five planes.
Total weight = 12g
Diameter = 45–50mm
Time = 10 minutes

Step 2: Binding the Cork
The cork pieces are placed inside an old felt cover and bound tightly with cotton string to hold them together. At this stage the core is hammered into shape using a mallet and a wooden horse to compress the cork and help it to form the required shape.
Total weight = 22–28g
Diameter = 45–50mm
Time = 6 minutes

Step 3: Binding the Cotton Webbing
Seven metres of cotton webbing is wrapped around the cork and felt core at as high a tension as is physically possible to achieve by hand. The ball is twisted through a small angle to evenly distribute the cotton. Using a fine waxed thread, the core is bound, by hand, under tension forming a complex shape of equilateral triangles, each side around 15mm in length. The total weight of the cotton is roughly 3g.
Total weight = 61g
Diameter = 59mm
Time = 10 minutes

Step 4: Covering the Ball
Melton felt is cut into two interlocking pieces in figure of eight shapes. These felt covers are then fixed over the core using 8mm tacks and stitched together by hand using a cotton thread.
Time = 22 minutes

The finished ball should be between 62mm and 65mm in diameter and between 71g and 78g in weight. It will have taken an average of 48 minutes to make.[87]

The purpose of this meticulous study, conducted by the Cambridge University Engineering Department, was to investigate the possibility of creating a manufactured ball. In addition to the technical analysis, the researchers surveyed 147 tennis players about their thoughts on an artificial ball. The vast majority of the respondents were highly resistant to any change. Most agreed that the seam should be hand-stitched, that the inconsistent bounce should remain, and that a handmade ball suited the image of the game. Tennis players, it is clear, are traditionalists. But even more striking was the breakdown of the data by people's handicap. Over 70% of weaker players (handicaps over 40) agreed that the ball inconsistencies should remain, whereas only around 25% of stronger players (handicaps below 9) were of the same opinion.[90]

What accounts for this discrepancy? Surely if you were not such a great player you would want to make the game easier for yourself by having a ball that bounced consistently. Obviously not: it seems that they would rather enjoy the traditions, and the apparent status attached to those traditions, than become better players or have better quality rallies. In contrast, a player of higher standard may be more immersed in playing the sport in ideal conditions than in basking in the glory of its quirky ancient traditions.

Neither of these groups is probably that concerned about the consequences for the working lives of professionals. The time professionals spend making balls could probably be better spent giving lessons, stringing rackets or training. On the other hand, a manufactured ball might reduce the need for having an assistant – who usually does most of the ball-making – leading to redundancies.

In recent years, some ball production has been outsourced to Haiti and India. This development appears to raise few ethical dilemmas for tennis players, most of whom seem uninterested in whether the new ball-makers receive a living wage or enjoy basic labour rights. Tennis does not yet have a fair trade ball.

THEATRE

In the seventeenth century, tennis courts were increasingly used as theatres and as a venue for plays, operas, ballet, circuses and other public entertainment. The courts were a perfect solution to the lack of purpose-built theatres at the time, particularly in France. In the beginning visiting troupes would erect makeshift stages, having a raised platform supported by trestles or wine casks at one end of the court. Most of the audience stood on the court, while more expensive tickets were available for those who wished to sit in the dedans or galleries, which functioned as boxes. Gradually some courts were totally refurbished and transformed into permanent theatres with pits, amphitheatres and boxes.

These tennis court theatres were often rowdy venues, and fights frequently broke out amongst members of the audience, sometimes involving the actors themselves. In one famous incident in Le Mans, the actors arrived without their costumes so borrowed the clothes of two young men who were busy playing tennis. After finishing their game they were furious to discover their garments being worn by the actors. The more angry of the two players struck one actor over the head with his racket and swords were drawn in the ensuing fight.[91]

Tennis courts played a significant role in popularising drama amongst common folk throughout France, and also in England, the Low Countries, Germany and Sweden, where courts were transformed into theatres. There was, additionally, an unexpected architectural outcome of the association: 'People became so accustomed to the fusion of the theatre with the tennis-court that eventually by force of association

THE FIRST BEAUTIFUL GAME

theatres came to be built in the shape of tennis-courts [in France]. From the sixteenth century onwards, in England, Italy and elsewhere, the semicircular shape prevailed; but France was to provide the exception, and the reason for this is attributable to the extraordinary popularity of her national game'.[92]

WORDPLAY

It may be that clues to explain the early development and popularity of tennis lie in the origins of the word 'tennis' itself. Yet this remains one of the great mysteries of the sport. Although they have been searching since the seventeenth century, no lexicographers or etymologists have yet provided a satisfactory derivation. Amongst the often bizarre and historically inaccurate suggestions are the following:

- ☞ It is from the French noun *tente*, because the game could have originally been played in tents.

- ☞ It is related to the Old High German *tenni*, a 'threshing floor', on which the game may have been played.

- ☞ It is connected to the sunken Nile metropolis of Tinnis.

- ☞ It originates from Tennois or Sennois, in the district of Champagne, where the game was popular.

- ☞ It comes from *tamis*, the French for sieve, and relates to the ball bouncing off a sieve to begin a point.

- ☞ It is based on *tainía* (tape), a reference to the tape or net separating the players.

- ☞ It is from the word *ten* as the game used to involve ten players.

FROM ABBOTS TO ZEALOTS

The most likely explanation, according to the Oxford English Dictionary, is that it originated in the medieval term *tenez!* (from the French, meaning 'hold!', 'mark!' or 'beware!'), which the serving player would shout out when they served to indicate that the ball was in play.[93]

ZEALOTS

The most notable characteristic of tennis players is their extraordinary zeal and fanaticism. This is reflected in their obsessive interest in the differing dimensions of tennis courts, as almost no two courts are geometric equals. In particular, tennis players love discussing the angle of the tambour jutting out from the main wall at the hazard end of the court. On some courts the angle is very sharp, on others the tambour is 'thinner'. The fascination with angles and dimensions is evident in tennis books from the sixteenth century to the present, such as the four-page table at the end of *A History of Tennis* by E. B. Noel and J. O. M. Clark, published in 1924. The table (*overleaf*) allows the reader to compare lengths, heights and angles on 55 different courts around the world.[94] If you find yourself captivated by these numbers, if they make you dream of new serves and strategies, if they make your palms sweat in excited anticipation of playing on the courts you've never visited, if they make you mourn the loss of some of these courts, then you may have understood what it is to be a tennis player.

Yet the zeal of a tennis player is not based merely on an appreciation of statistics. The game is also played because it is fun. Concepts such as 'fun' or 'joy' are difficult to define and explain. One of the most significant theories of enjoyment is that developed by the psychologist Mihaly Csikszentmihalyi. Through studying rock climbers, basketball players and chess players, he found that they all sometimes experience a feeling that he calls 'flow,' which is a 'holistic sensation that people feel

	Hampton Court.	Lord's (New Court).	Queen's Club (2 Courts).	Cheveley, Newmarket	Prince's Club.	Knightsbridge.	Oxford, Merton Street.
	ft. in.	ft. in.	ft. in.	ft. in.	ft. in.	ft. in.	ft. in.
Greatest internal length including Penthouses	110.11	110.0	..	110.4	..	112.0	103.9½
Greatest internal breadth including Penthouses	39.7	38.8	..	38.10	..	38.0	36.8½
Length of Floor	96.3	96.0½	96.8	96.4	96.4	96.5½	93.0
Breadth of Floor at Dedans Wall	32.1¾	31.8	31.3	31.10	31.7	31.10	29.10
Breadth of Floor at Grille Wall	30.6	30.2	29.9	30.2	29.9½	30.1½	28.6
Play line at sides	18.8½ at Tambour 18.5½	18.0	18.0	18.0	..	18.6	17.0
Play line at ends	23.10	23.0	23.0	24.0	..	23.6	27.0
Height to ceilings or beams	31.9	30.0	..	30.0	..	..	27.0
Height of Penthouse, upper edge	10.5	10.7	10.6	10.0	10.0	11.1½	9.2½
Height of Penthouse, lower edge	7.2	7.1½	7.2	7.2	7.2½	7.5	6.9
Width of Penthouse over Galleries	7.5	7.0	7.9	7.0	7.9	8.0	5.10½
Width of Penthouse over Grille	7.4	7.0	7.9	7.0	7.9	8.0	5.4
Width of Penthouse over Dedans	7.4	7.0	7.9	7.0	7.9	8.0	5.5¼
Height—Floor to lower edge of Galleries	3.5½	3.8	3.8	3.7	3.8	3.8½	3.6⅛
Height—Floor to lower edge of Grille	3.7½	3.8	3.8	3.7	3.8	3.8½	3 5¾

when they act with total involvement' that is not usually accessible in everyday life. The flow state is partly defined by what it is not: it is not boring and it does not raise anxiety or worry. In positive terms, it is when experience seems to flow from one action to the next, where you feel in control of your actions, and where there is little distinction between self and environment, between stimulus and response, or between past, present and future. Flow can be experienced by top professional athletes, amateur squash players, surgeons performing delicate operations or participants in a yoga or meditation session.[95] In sporting contexts it is a feeling often described as being 'in the zone'. There is no doubt that a tennis match can induce this sensation of 'flow,' where the feeling of joy derives from a sense of total involvement and immersion in the present moment, where worries and cares seem to dissolve into nothingness.

Another approach is that we derive joy from activities that are in some way magical or make-believe, that are an escape from the seriousness, strains or boredom of ordinary life.[96]

The tennis court may be such a magical world. Although this conflicts with the idea that tennis reflects the reality of battle situations or competitive struggles for survival, it accords with the experience of zealous players through the ages who have always loved the quirkiness of their game. When on a tennis court you feel enclosed in a strange realm of buttresses and sloping roofs, variously shaped and positioned targets, surprising angles, bizarre rules. Just as children play games in invented worlds, adults have used tennis to enter an equivalent unreality. Perhaps the ultimate appeal of tennis is that it remains one of the great theatres of the imagination.

※

What does this curious history of tennis tell us about human beings? Perhaps that we are warriors re-enacting battles as well as worriers evading stress and anxiety; we are violent and angry but we are also bored; we crave risk and tension while seeking refinement and attention; we are the products of both medieval society and capitalist ideology; we want to immerse ourselves in the moment and be transported into make-believe. Tennis reveals us as creations of nature and nurture, and individual and collective histories. We are untidy bundles of memory, desire and contradiction.

3 *Life in Court*

What's the best thing about being a tennis pro?
'Playing tennis. What's the best thing about life? Playing tennis. Yeah, that's what I think. Life is a tennis court. I'm never happier than when I'm playing a proper match - you can erase everything in life.'

This is life according to Wayne Davies, tennis obsessive and World Champion from 1987 to 1994. He told me how, following his split from his wife in 1985, he effectively moved into the tennis club in New York, where he was at the time Head Professional. His life became totally bounded by the world of tennis:

When you were in New York, did you have friends outside tennis?
'No. No interest.'
So did you have much of a social life?
'None.'
None?
'Why? I only had one aim.'

Wayne slept on a mattress above the club swimming pool. Living at the court left him all the time he needed to practise and achieve his ambition of becoming the world's greatest player. 'All I did was spend time training', he said. 'I used to get up at six o'clock in the morning and train from 6.30 till 10 every day, religiously, for years and years, and then start work at 10.30.' Sometimes he would even practise in the middle of the night. His dedication was absolute: 'If you're going to get good at anything, you know, you've got to have tunnel vision. I could never understand why all the other pros would go and play golf – why practise your golf swing when your forehand

Wayne Davies at Hampton Court Palace in 1987.[97]

sucks? I could never understand why people would waste their competitiveness on a game of Monopoly or whatever. I couldn't care . . . you've only got so much nervous energy.'

I could sense his nervous energy. He was fidgety, excitable and speaking incredibly quickly, his mind darting around just as he does when on court. For over twenty years this energy has been almost totally focused on tennis, every aspect of it. Small, skinny and wearing large, square goofy glasses, you would not suspect that he is a remarkable athlete.

✫

Where does it come from, the extraordinary passion, dedication, obsession, ambition? Wayne grew up in Victoria, Australia, in the city of Geelong. He attended local government schools, where he displayed a self-confidence that some considered arrogance: 'I was a Smart Alec, that would categorise me. At school I was straight A's all the time, and I got suspended for talking too much! I used to get into so much trouble because I was just bored. The teachers hated it when you were just messing around and they ask you a question and you knew the answer straight away. I'm not saying I'm any genius, but the people I was at school with were not exactly the smartest people on earth. I was also the top chemist in the state – I got the CSIRO Bowen Prize. I was always prepared. Something that's always categorised me, I think, I'm always prepared. If I'm going to do something, I mightn't be able to achieve it, but it's not because I haven't done the groundwork.'

Wayne has been a fanatical and exceptional sportsman since his youth. Originally obsessed with Aussie Rules – a spectacular derivative of football and rugby – he later became a top squash player: 'I was really good at sport. That's all I ever did, dreamed of playing on Saturday. And I hated going to church – my parents were Methodists – because the only time you could ever get any coaching was on a Sunday morning. As a result, I hate church. All because it stopped me playing sport. That's true! Aussie Rules was my favourite sport. I was more than handy at the game, but I was just too small, came out being very injured. When I was about 20 I had to throw it in, because my knees, even then, were getting crushed. About then, too, I'd taken up squash, and I quickly progressed through there. In Geelong I was easily the best player, and it was a pretty big city – a quarter of a million people.' Almost nothing could distract him from sport: 'Women, for example, I couldn't care less about them till I was much older. They were nothing to do with football or squash or whatever, they were useless. It's not that I actually thought in that fashion, but I excluded it subconsciously.'

After leaving school, Wayne became a high school science teacher, living with his then wife in the countryside near Geelong. He discovered tennis at the Royal Melbourne Tennis Club, which he had been invited to join to play squash: 'I was 23 on September 13th, 1978, when I played my first ever game of tennis. There was like déjà vu, seriously, going on in the court, religious experience. I played against Lesley Ronaldson and she thrashed me! And I remember, I walked up to Chris Ronaldson [Lesley's husband and then a professional at the Melbourne court] and I said, "I want as many games as I need to beat her".

Not Wayne's style: Mr J. M. Heathcote, British Amateur Champion 1888, gently cutting the ball.[98]

Wayne's style: leaping for a forehand volley in the early 1980s, viewed through the side gallery netting.[99]

Absolutely that! That's exactly what I wanted to do. And I never played her again. But after six hits, I was more . . . I guess my handicap after six hits would have been well and truly low twenties. And I only played about a dozen times between then and taking up the Assistant Tennis Professional job.'

So Wayne resigned from his job at the school, took a huge salary cut and became a tennis professional: 'I remember riding my motorcycle for 45 minutes to the train station at Geelong, then taking the train for an hour and a half to Melbourne, then taking a bus for 20 minutes to the Melbourne Tennis Club, and being there by eight o'clock in the morning each day. Oh, Jesus, it was just a nightmare, that kind of stuff! If I was going to work in Melbourne, that's what I had to do.'

✣

He was (and still is) possessed with an extraordinary self-assurance and hunger to win. Looking around at the other club pros, he was convinced that 'I'll be able to smash these guys in two years!'. And his predication almost came true. Within that period he beat Colin Lumley and Lachie Deuchar, but failed to defeat Chris Ronaldson, who was soon to become World Champion. He described with characteristic irreverence how he was soon able to 'beat the shit' out of all the top players in the United States, and most of those in the United Kingdom.

Wayne had decided to play tennis his own way. Ignoring the classical formula of playing controlled cut (sliced) shots into the corners of the court, he astonished the tennis world with his unbelievably aggressive play. 'I'm on court with all these top players and my philosophy was, "These guys can rally more than me – they've been playing longer! It's so obvious, it takes skill to do that. So I'm not going to do that, I'm just going to hit the ball as hard as I can." And that's what I did. And people would say to me, "You can't do that", "You can't do this", "You'll never be any good", "It's just not tennis". Who cares? There's a lot of pressure on you to play pretty, isn't there? And I just creamed it. Creamed it. I just kept breaking their rackets. I remember playing [English professional] Frank Willis. And I'm 6-1, 6-0, and 1-0 up – and he motions me to come to the net, so I thought, "All right". He says to me, "Wayne, you've got to cut the ball!" I'll never forget that. These guys had no idea! Ibsen wrote, in *A Public Enemy*, "The majority is always wrong", and I agree with that.'

'You're talking about a guy who was really skinny too. I would have been 135 pounds. But I could run like the wind – being highly ranked in squash, I was very, very fit and fast, and I was always pressing forward, like in cricket. So I'd just move into it and take it on the chin. I exuded confidence. Soon I was the number two player in the world.'

After six months Wayne left the Melbourne club to take up

a position in Hobart, Tasmania. Soon he was offered the job of Head Professional in France, at the club in Bordeaux, which was followed by a short stint at Hampton Court. The prestigious and elite all-male New York Racquet and Tennis Club then asked Wayne to become their Head Professional in 1982. The club was used to having one of the world's top players as their pro – Pierre Etchebaster, World Champion for three decades until the mid-1950s, had worked there for most of his career. It was obvious that Wayne had the potential to take the World Championship off Chris Ronaldson, which he finally managed in 1987. He was to stay at the New York club for thirteen years.

During Wayne's early years as a professional, his passion for tennis and desire for sporting glory transformed into obsession: 'I couldn't care about anything else. "You know nothing about tennis? Don't talk to me. Go away".' Unsurprisingly, his relationships outside the tennis world suffered. I asked him how his wife reacted to his focus on tennis: 'No idea . . . when it comes to my tennis, I don't think anything got in the way of that. And like it or lump it, you know . . . we discussed it, of course, but it was no . . . I think it was sort of more a one-way discussion. I can't remember. I really can't remember. And it's not that I think that I've purged it from my memory cells! In Bordeaux I was living in a garage, literally, next door to the court. That's where the big rift came between my wife and I. She hated it. I loved it! I was moving into new worlds and I was involved in dealing with people all the time, and there she was, pregnant and missing home, and all those things that went right over my head at the time.'

*

Wayne is not only a rebel on the court, reflected in his unorthodox style. He is also one off the court. Over the years he has shown more contempt than most professionals for the amateur elite who have traditionally controlled the game. In his view they have attempted to limit opportunities for professional players, particularly the introduction of better working conditions and pay, and more tournament prize money. 'It's us against them,' he says, 'us, the pros, against them, the amateurs'.

He remembered what it was like working in Melbourne: 'There's a phrase I've heard, that rings in my ears. I hear Committee people saying, out loud, "Oh, we compensate them adequately". Everything's always adequate. I was told to call everyone 'Mister', and straightaway I said, "Well, beat it. I'm not going to do this. If somebody earns my respect, then I'll call them 'Mister'." I was absolutely determined to be rebellious if I thought our rights were being trodden on. I hope I never change, you know, call a spade a spade.' What do you think you were rebelling against? I then asked him: 'Erm . . . that's a good question. Imposed structure. I could easily see that the job we were doing was a lifeline of the club. The pros are really everything, without the pros it just doesn't exist, and I don't think that our input, then, was at all recognised. I went to the club and I said, "Look, I'm married. I'm this, I'm that. I'm getting $10,000 a year. What do you see my position to be here? Am I going to be always Assistant Pro?" And they said, "We can't answer that". So within six months I left.'

'What got me into most trouble was reacting, in print, against what I saw were really super injustices. Little publications came out that I had a hand in. Many times clubs have promised things to the professionals and haven't delivered, and I've pointed it out to every club in the world when that happens. A good example is when a club held a tournament. I was playing in the final and we couldn't use the court because it was too slippery, it was too sweaty. So we had to delay for eight hours and ended up playing at seven o'clock at night. I won. And they said, "Okay, we're going to charge eight hours at non-members prices – $40 an hour – we'll take $320 off the prize money". I then wrote down that they were thieves, and circulated it round the whole world. It's a true story, and I embarrassed them.'

The former World Champion is also renowned for his juvenile antics and pranks, an extension of his rebellious character and irreverent independence. When banned from using a particular brand of racket when playing in the US early in his career, he turned up for his match at the conservative New York club wearing a pink bandana and carrying a bright pink racket with a white skull and crossbones on it. This was the Andre Agassi of real tennis. On another occasion he was asked to mark (umpire) an important tournament match. The officials insisted that he mark standing at the net post even though Wayne protested that it was too dangerous, having recently been knocked out by a ball when doing so. But he had no choice. His response was to perform his duties wearing flip-flops, pink swimming trunks, and nothing else. 'That was funny,' he recalled. 'The guy there came and just tore strips off me – "That's the worst thing I've ever seen". It was their fault but, typically, I sort of . . . over-react a bit. I should have just said, "Okay", turned round and gone home.'

My favourite story, illustrating his remorseless sense of humour, is the following: 'I was having a haircut – there's a full-time barber at the New York club – and I was half way through my haircut, and this member comes rushing in, and just tries to pull me out of my seat. "Buddy, just relax. Go change. We'll be finished in five minutes". So he gets the Manager, and the Manager had to act like I had to go – but he winked at me. So, all right. The other guy has his hair cut, I come back, finish my haircut. Then I trot down to the bank, get out a hundred bucks, run up to the third floor again and go up to the changing room attendants there, who get the clothing out. I said, "You see that guy there?" They said, "Yeah". "Here's a hundred bucks. There's another hundred coming for you every six months". Now, members there, they love having their cubicles really close to where they run in. So

I said, "All right. This is what's going to happen, and I'll come and check. He now has to go from being at the front, to being way up the back. And you're never going to wash his clothes again. You can dry them, by all means. But you're never washing them". So they didn't. They stank. The beauty of it was me just chuckling to myself every time he passed by. If you treat an employee badly – the guy who does the grunt work – he'll get you.'

*

Like many players, Wayne loves the history of tennis: 'I've read everything you can read, know all the matches'. He would walk onto court with his opponent and say things like, 'Do you realise that 120 years ago today Peter Latham played so and so on this court and lost seven sets to three?'. His real tennis website has a 'fantasy' match section that describes invented encounters between great players of the past. His obsession with the history extends to his personal life – his son Jay is named after early twentieth century tennis champion Jay Gould.

> 'In front of 150 members, the 8th of Pierre's Championship defences began with Pierre serving his characteristic railroad. Control of length at tight moments requires nerves of steel, and Johnson seemed to let the occasion get the better of him during the first set. Frequent loose balls off the back-wall set up telling cross court winners for Pierre, whose footwork in the corners was impeccable. 1st set Pierre 6-2.
>
> Towards the end of the set it was noticeable that Johnson was forsaking his normal length game for that of hitting firmly to the back-wall/nick area. This set frequent chases, nearly all of which Pierre beat after changing ends. It did

have the effect, however, of letting Johnson overcome his emotions and start imposing more of his will. Consequently the game started to pick up pace rapidly, and the younger man began hitting more and more outright winners. The second set was remarkable for how many long rallies were controlled by Pierre, only to see him finally lose them to a forceful shot from his opponent. 2nd set Johnson 6-4.'

> *An extract from the 'Fantasy Tennis' page of Wayne's tennis website. Here he invents a match between World Champion Pierre Etchebaster and challenger Jack Johnson, held at the New York club in 1953. The match, according to Wayne's imagination, went on for three days.*[100]

Wayne's own matches are now part of that history. He revels in his victories but remembers them with his special brand of humility: 'One of the best matches I've ever played is winning the US Open Doubles in 1986, with Peter de Svastich against Chris Ronaldson and Barry Toates, because I played unbelievably well. It was 6-5 in the fifth set. I won the last game with two dedans and a winning gallery. It was great! That one sticks out, not the World Championship, oddly enough – it wasn't as good a performance. I don't think I'm that good, and if I don't think *I'm* that good, well, certainly my contemporaries aren't. You see, I know we're just big fish in a small pond. I think if the really good players took the game up, the ball would just be thumped left, right and centre. Some 6' 8" guy who can move like a cat would just nail the ball every single time.'

Although he could recall the victories, often point by point, he seemed almost too keen to explain away the losses that taint his record: 'I shouldn't have played the 1985 World Championship. I'd just split up from my wife, I wasn't ready to play, I got thrashed 7-1 by Chris Ronaldson. I just embarrassed myself and shouldn't have played. My other regret was Rob Fahey beat me in '94. I was three sets to one down after

Wayne (left) in the late 1990s, still able to smile after his losses to Chris Ronaldson (centre) and Rob Fahey (right).[101]

the first day. Then I finally found a serve, and some great play in the first set next day, and won 6-2. It wasn't that I was playing out of my skin, I was playing very controlled stuff, and I knew I was either going to win three sets to one or four-love that day. That's three sets to two at this stage, on his home court. I'm playing fantastic, and he'd gone, I thought. You could see the fear. And the first serve of the next set, I pulled my back out. And it goes down in the record books as 7-2. I hate that!'

In recent years Wayne's main goal was to have the record number of appearances in the World Championship final, something that he achieved despite suffering from severe knee problems and a double fracture in his lower vertebrae. But he is afraid of going on too long, of his glory being tarnished. 'People only remember your last performance,' he said. 'I don't see myself being the old soldier who doesn't die, who just drifts, just fades away – I don't think that's going to be me.'

*

When I spoke to him he was running the new court in Sydney that he had helped establish. The club, which opened in 1997, was struggling financially. He told me how he was not interested in building another court: 'It's too much hard work. And I'm not interested in furthering anybody's causes in it, you know . . . there's no reflected glory to bask in.' He was absolutely certain that he could use his skills as a professional to make the club a success: 'I'm great at it! I am great at what I do. I have never got stale. You can feel it. Look, I've always been very aware of myself, and I know I'm great there.'

Over the years his knees had been destroyed by playing and he was about to have another operation. But he was still on court practising, attempting to invent new ways of hitting the ball that would accommodate his growing physical limitations. Then in his forties, Wayne was still one of the world's top players, using his incredibly aggressive play, unorthodox style and competitive determination to maintain his position.

He was intent on proving to me that he was still a champion. After we'd spoken he asked me to stand at one end of the court and hit him balls as hard as I could to anywhere on the court and he would attempt to return them. I thought this would be too easy for me – I'd hit the ball straight into targets like the grille or blast it low into the back wall so it would be rolling along the floor by the time he started moving to it. He returned almost every ball. His speed and anticipation were astonishing.

We returned to the club room and Wayne launched into a discourse on the need for aggressive play, especially the return of serve deflected off the main wall into the dedans, which automatically wins you the point. 'You only have to read a bit, and Lukin – in his 1822 book, *A Treatise on Tennis* – says that the shot that can't be practised too much is the main wall force.'

*

'I love the game,' mused Wayne. 'I've always had such a blast doing it, because I'm doing my own thing while still fulfilling my job requirements. No one's getting more enthusiastic than me about it, I don't believe, and I know so much about it, I really do. I'm one of the learned few. People criticise me for being a sort of crackpot or over the top. It's the tall poppy syndrome, isn't it? And so I don't care.'

*

Wayne's passion for tennis is extraordinary. He loves the game. He is obsessed. He sacrificed his previous career, his social life and his first marriage to achieve his ambition of becoming the world's greatest player. By focusing on one thing he has developed his talents and potential to their fullest, while being innovative and creative at the same time. He has absorbed tennis and tennis has absorbed him. He is a slave, though a willing one. Life is a tennis court, said Wayne.

I often wonder whether I lack ambition, both on the tennis court and in life in general. I have avoided traditional career paths and am more interested in developing a variety of skills than in focusing on mastering any single one. I would rather go for a walk on a beautiful morning than attain fame and fortune. What would Wayne think about my life? Would he condemn me for lacking ambition? I try to imagine how I would be judged.

*

'All arise'. The announcement is made by a court clerk in ochre pantaloons and a red velvet coat. He wears a short wig with curls that echo the frills on the shirt emerging through his coat. His eyes are wide and placid, his nose long and kinked. He looks curiously familiar. We all stand up as the judge walks into the courtroom. The judge, too, is dressed strangely, in long white trousers and a white cardigan with blue striped piping. Instead of a wig he wears a beret. His face is stern, his mouth taut and curved down, like an upside down smile. He takes his seat, as do the rest of us. 'Mr Justice Etchebaster presiding,' declares the clerk.

Pierre Etchebaster, in his favourite cardigan, ready to serve judgement (left).[102] *Raymond Masson, a stately court clerk* (right).[103]

I suddenly understand. The court clerk is Raymond Masson, tennis World Champion in 1765. And His Honour is Pierre Etchebaster, undefeated World Champion from 1928 to 1955. Then I look around. We are not in a normal courtroom. This is a tennis court. I see the sloping roofs of the penthouse, the tambour jutting out from the main wall, the gallery openings on the opposite wall. On one side of the net is a rabble of seated individuals wearing the tennis clothing of different historical epochs, each fiddling with a racket. On the opposite side, where I am, sits the judge, the clerk, stenographers, lawyers, a jury. I am seated in a small boxed-off area, slightly apart from the others.

'Will the accused stand,' says Masson the clerk. Nobody moves. 'Will the accused please stand up,' he repeats loudly. Nobody moves. He turns around and glares at me. I look behind me. Nothing but the wall. 'Mr Krznaric,' I hear the judge say, 'you are required to be upstanding for this part of the proceedings.' Me? I lift myself up hesitantly, my palms are suddenly sweating. Masson approaches me, holding a book. He takes my hand and places it on top of the book, which has a green cover and two crossed tennis rackets on the front. It's *The Annals of Tennis* by Julian Marshall, the 1878 classic that is the great bible of the game. 'Do you swear to tell the truth, the whole truth and nothing but the truth?' After replying, 'I do,' I remove my hand, relieved that it hasn't left a sweaty stain on the cover.

A figure on the other side of the court now rises and walks into the open space in the middle of the service end, around the line representing 'chase six yards'. His head is down, his hands behind his back, he is wearing a shiny white and blue tracksuit. He approaches me slowly then lifts his head. Big square glasses cover his face. It's Wayne Davies.

'Life is a tennis court,' Wayne begins. 'And the pathetic individual standing before you today has absolutely no understanding of this. The prosecution believes he has committed two crimes. First, this bloke lacks passion for the game. He just doesn't really care about it. For him, it's another little hobby, not a way of life. And his second crime: insufficient ambition as a player. Just look at him – it's bloody obvious if you ask me. There's no fire in his eyes.' He pauses for effect. The crowd on the other side of the net murmurs, then begins to erupt. 'Shame! Shame!' I hear the words echoing and bouncing off the black walls of the court.

'Silence!' roars out the judge. The sound dies out. Wayne resumes his speech, now facing the jury. 'Yes, this man has disgraced the game and it's time for him to be punished. The penalty for these combined offences, jurors, is to be banned from playing forever. And he deserves it – make him suffer! If you decide he's only guilty of one of these crimes, you have the right to take ten points off his handicap, which currently stands at 1.5. Yes, you may reduce him to a miserable handicap of 11.5 for the remainder of his natural life!' I am stunned. Banned from playing?! A permanent handicap of 11.5? How could they possibly do this to me? I haven't lost a match to anyone with a handicap of 11.5 for over a decade! It just wouldn't be fair.

'That isn't fair!' I say loudly. 'I haven't done anything wrong. I love tennis. This is ridiculous.' The judge interrupts me: 'Mr Krznaric, I must ask you to respect the rules of the court. Prosecutor Davies has not yet finished his opening speech.' I am silenced. How could I possibly challenge the instructions of the great Pierre Etchebaster? I stare upwards. Facing me, on the wall above the side penthouse, are the words 'Life is a tennis court' written in huge letters. The prosecutor turns towards the judge, pulling a small booklet from his pocket and waving it in the air. 'We all know, don't we, that these crimes are clearly stated in the Tennis and Rackets Association Rulebook. The guy's a criminal, pure and simple.' The jurors, some of whom are busy sewing the covers on tennis balls, nod their heads up and down in silent approval. Wayne turns to me, spitting out his next words: 'Buddy, you're in for it now.'

'Mr Krznaric, would you like to make any opening remarks? says the judge solemnly. I stand up, I'm feeling nervous. 'Yes, M'lud . . . I would like to give you, and the respectable members of the jury, some examples of my passion for tennis. Furthermore, I wish to illustrate how, since I first discovered the game when at university in 1989, it has been an integral part of my life.' I am speaking a little too pompously. Just tell it like it is, I think to myself.

'To begin, as a student I would go to the tennis court at seven each morning, before it officially opened, to practise alone. In winter I wore fingerless gloves to keep out the cold. While living in an Essex village I bought a car for the sole purpose of getting to the nearest court, in Cambridge, even though I don't like cars and I find driving frightening. I regularly left at dawn, driving two and a half hours in total to practise for an hour before work. When travelling around Australia I detoured hundreds of miles so I could play at Ballarat in Victoria.'

I stop for a moment. Everyone is listening. I decide to go on: 'I now live in Oxford, five minutes cycle from a court, and practise three or four times a week. In season I travel to tournaments and league matches most weekends. The first thing I do on Monday mornings is turn on my computer to reserve courts on the club's online booking system. The little money I earn, I spend on tennis. I am currently obsessed with the question of how my non-aggressive and conciliatory personality off the court limits my ability to make my style of play less timid and more forceful. I've also been reading books on neuroscience to discover whether practising a particular shot in my head at night might improve that same shot in reality through stimulating and "training" my neural pathways. My experiments of applying ideas of movement and balance in the Alexander Technique are ongoing. Last night I dreamed about playing.'

The words keep coming. I find it easy to tell the truth: 'On a teaching trip to Venice in 1999 I spent each afternoon searching for the remains of old tennis courts. I eventually found a high wall in an ancient courtyard with a buttress jutting out exactly like a tambour on a tennis court. Overjoyed at my discovery I took dozens of photos from every possible angle. People watched me, perplexed. I recently visited a friend in Brighton who I hadn't seen in three years. The first thing we did together, at my request, was to search for the remains of the old court in Little Preston Street. The walls of my study are covered with tennis prints and photos. I am even writing a book on tennis. My bicycle is named after former World Champion Chris Ronaldson . . . And that car I bought in Essex, it was called . . . Pierre Etchebaster.'

'*Mon Dieu!*' cries out the judge. 'Is this true, Mr Prosecutor?'

'Er – well, yes,' replies Wayne, uncharacteristically sheepish.

'Then why is this respectable young man on trial, I ask you?! There is no doubt that he is a tennis fanatic of the most reputable kind. Rarely have I ever encountered such an uncompromising love for this sport. Mr Davies, do you have any witnesses who can prove that he lacks passion for our beautiful game?'

'Yes I do, Your Honour.'

The court clerk arises and announces, 'Bring forth the first witness.'

A bearded man wearing workmen's overalls and a woollen hat emerges from the opening onto the court at the net post. He takes a seat opposite me. My God, it's Mike Abbott.

'Mr Abbott,' says Wayne, once again pacing around the service end. 'Mr Abbott, you've met this fella before, haven't you?' Wayne points a finger at me.

'Yes,' he replies, not looking me in the eye.

'I want you to tell this courtroom about what Mr Krznaric was doing between May 15 and May 20, 2004.'

'Well,' Mike begins, 'Roman – sorry, Mr Krznaric – was attending one of my green woodworking courses in Gloucestershire that week.'

'And what, pray, is "green woodworking"?' interrupts the judge.

'It's an ancient technique of making furniture and other items using fresh, rather than seasoned timber. We chop down some trees, then the course participants cut and cleave the wood, and make a ladderback chair using traditional methods and tools, such as the pole lathe. Mr Krznaric spent the week making an ash armchair with a woven wych elm bark seat.'

The judge now addresses himself to the prosecuting lawyer: 'Mr Davies, I cannot see the relevance of this witness to the case.'

'Take it easy, Your Honour. I'm just getting there . . . Mr Abbott, during this week of so-called "green woodworking" did the accused ever mention that he played tennis?'

'Not that I remember, sir,' says Mike.

'You mean that he never uttered a word about the game? Not even once?'

'I don't recall him ever doing so. No. I'd never heard of real tennis until I came here today.'

'That'll be all, mate,' says Wayne in his clipped Australian accent.

Mike Abbott is taken from the room.

'It's all pretty obvious now, isn't it?' resumes Wayne to the room. 'This guy who says he's so passionate about the game didn't say a word about it for six full days. Jurors – is this the behaviour of a tennis fanatic? You must be kidding. Look, in twenty years I haven't gone a single day without talking about the game. If you care about it, you're going to talk about it. And one thing's for sure – you wouldn't be pissing about doing this "green woodworking" stuff. You'd be on court practising your forehand volley or your railroad service! He obviously doesn't know the meaning of passion.' The jury nod idiotically.

'Do you have anything to say in your defence?' asks the judge, turning towards me. I have to think quickly.

'I do, Your Honour . . . It is true that I didn't mention tennis during the week in Gloucestershire. But I was – albeit unintentionally – learning about tennis while on the course. When I returned home I was looking at some eighteenth century tennis drawings that appear in Garsault's book on tennis, *Art du Paumier-Raquetier et de la Paume*. In one illustration there are three tennis professionals making rackets and sewing balls. They are using the very same tools and methods that I learned about on the woodworking course. One, for instance, is using a draw knife to shave back a racket handle. I had never even heard of a draw knife, let alone used one, before taking the course! In another drawing there appears a low elongated stool called a shaving horse, one of the main workshop items for the *paumier*, the tennis professional . . . but also for the green

Gloucestershire, twenty-first century.[104]

France, eighteenth century.[105]

woodworker. On returning from the course I looked at my tennis rackets more closely than I ever had before, studying their construction, the layering of the wood, the direction of the grain. Without taking the furniture course I would never have noticed all these details. So I discovered, miraculously, that one of my passions was providing new insights and understanding about the other.'

'Ah yes, of course . . . ' The judge leans back in his chair, staring into the distance, reminiscing: 'The shaving horse, I remember them from my days in Paris, what we called the *chevalet á placer les échalas*. Most interesting.' Wayne is fidgety, obviously desperate to say something. He stands up and blurts out: 'But what was he doing on this course in the first place? He couldn't care less about tennis!'

'Order! order!' shouts the judge, who has returned to the present. He pounds his gavel – which is actually an old tennis racket with a broken string – onto his bench. 'Wait your turn Mr Davies.'

My confidence is increasing and I am determined to continue. 'Your honour, I would like to call forth my own first witness, Mr Ben Ronaldson'. I had spotted Ben amongst the spectators. Ben approaches the service end. He's looking scruffy as usual, scratchy beard, shirt hanging out. We've played each other often over recent years. He takes his place. I begin to speak, playing on the drama and formality of the occasion. 'Ladies and gentlemen of the jury, before you is a tennis player of undisputed pedigree. Born in 1976, Ben Ronaldson belongs to the most famous family in the game – his parents, Lesley and Chris, are both professionals and were the finest players in the world in their day. He spent most of his childhood and youth at tennis clubs, particularly at Hampton Court Palace. One period of absence from the tennis world was when he studied chemistry at Oxford University. But he gave it up and became a tennis pro. He is currently the Assistant Professional at Hampton Court Palace.' The room is quiet. Nobody knows exactly why I have chosen Ben Ronaldson from amongst the dozens of faces.

'Mr Ronaldson, could you describe to those present the extent of your passion for tennis?' I ask him. Ben shuffles a little awkwardly in his seat, pauses a moment, then launches into my question[106]: 'When you're on court playing, it's just so enjoyable. For instance, I had food poisoning when I was spending some time at Hatfield tennis club. I couldn't sit still. I could not sleep. The only thing I could do to avoid thinking about it, was playing tennis. I went out and played for five hours, because I was so ill. That really says it all to me, because

I really enjoy playing it so much. If a top player like Mike Gooding phoned me up and said, "Do you want to practise every morning at six o'clock?" I'd do it. I wouldn't know why, but it would actually be because I just enjoy hitting balls. I don't know if it's an instinct thing. Where has that come from? There is something built-in that's just fantastic about striking a tennis ball that you don't get in any other sport, not even golf. If you make a connection in golf, you feel lucky half the time. It's a very jarring action, there's something wrong with it. Whereas in real tennis, if you hit a ball clean on the strings, it's just nice. Having just listened to myself say that, I do sound a bit eccentric about the game, don't I!'

'Thank you very much, Mr Ronaldson. I think you have made it perfectly clear that you are remarkably passionate about tennis.' I pause and look around the room, trying to meet the gaze of all those present. 'Now, let me ask you another question . . . Do you have any other passions?' Instead of answering, Ben digs around in his pocket. But he's unable to find what he is searching for. He looks a little worried. So do I. Finally, he smiles, drawing out a pack of cards and holding them up to the judge and jury. And he says just what I hoped he would say: 'I'm a person who works on inspiration – in anything. Now I'm playing this card game, called Magic, where I'm in a team with the best player in England. I travel round different countries with them, playing in tournaments. Last weekend I was playing in Madrid. I'm doing better at this than I've ever done at anything else in my life, simply because I've got that inspiration. That's what I do in my spare time. In one room at home I've got millions of cards just laid out in different patterns. It's in Mensa's top five games, so I'm not lacking intellectual stimulation. I was: that was a problem I was having. Real tennis is not a very taxing job on the brain, and for someone like me – without trying to sound arrogant – I could not survive just with real tennis. You have to have interests elsewhere. In my opinion, it cannot be a life, unless you're expecting a really dull one.'

From facing Ben, I swivel around on my heels towards the jury. 'As you can see, Mr Ronaldson is passionate about tennis. But he has more than one passion. In his case it is a card game. In my case, I am passionate about furniture making. Mr Ronaldson's trip to Madrid was no different to my sojourn in the Gloucestershire woods. While I admire the absolute dedication that the prosecuting lawyer, Wayne Davies, has shown towards tennis throughout his career, I personally feel the need to seek a variety of experiences, to avoid the narrow specialisation of a single occupation or obsession that can blind you to new ways of looking at the world and new ways of appreciating it. I declare that I am not guilty of the crime of 'insufficient passion' for tennis, since it is no crime to care deeply about many things.'

I stop. And the crowd cheers as if I had just hit a brilliant forehand cross-court into the winning gallery. The judge takes off his beret, placing it on the bench. He has something to say: 'Indeed, I can appreciate your point, Roman. In my early days, before I was introduced to tennis in 1922, I was champion of all the Basque pelota ball sports – *main nue*, a kind of handball, *pala*, using wooden paddles, and *chistera*, where we used a large curved basket instead of a racket. In the following years I sometimes missed playing these other games. Each is beautiful in its own way. And there's no doubt we need many different experiences to learn about life. I fought on all the fronts of France for four years in the Great War, from the Somme to Verdun. I was eight days in Verdun, it was very bad. One night we slept on thousands of dead men . . .'[107] Pierre Etchebaster's voice trails off into his memory.

Wayne stands up again, now fuming: 'Pierre – Your Honour. Please. All Krznaric's done so far is blather on about trees and bicycles! It is now time to consider the second charge: lack of ambition as a player.'

'Very well, Monsieur Davies,' says Pierre, a little reluctantly.

'If you're going to get good at something, you've got to work at it,' Wayne states in a commanding tone. 'And I should know. I spent years training religiously to become World Champion. Now, Roman Krznaric is a pretty good player. But he could become a hell of a lot better if he was faster around the court and improved his footwork. The guy is just not fit, he's too slow. He knows it, yet he's never made the effort to do anything about it! Sure, he's practised on court a lot. But you never see him really training hard – he never goes to the gym, he doesn't go running. Now and then he paddles around in a swimming pool, doing a few laps, but he doesn't push himself. This guy just isn't serious about training and so isn't serious about becoming a top player. He isn't even serious about winning – I have countless witnesses who can recall him saying ridiculous things like, 'I don't care if I win or not, as long as I've played well by my own standards' or 'losing successfully is an art form' or 'I don't aim to "crush my opponents" – this isn't a fight or a war'. What a joker! Ambition naturally arises out of any true passion – the desire to achieve, to be the greatest. This is a man without drive, without ambition. He's the worst kind of criminal.' Wayne then faces the spectators and calls out to them: 'What has he got?'

'No ambition!' they cry out in unison.

'What has he got?' repeats the prosecutor. The crowd begins to chant:

'No ambition, no ambition, no ambition, no ambition'. Soon they are upstanding, bleating out the words.

In the whole room only one person, apart from myself, remains seated. He is amongst the spectators. Wearing a neat shirt, tie and knitted cardigan, he sits quietly, back upright, staring directly ahead. In his hands he holds not a tennis racket, but a large bow, with a quiver of arrows on his back. I have no idea how he got here but I sense he can help me. 'I would like to call forth a witness, Your Honour.' The judge isn't listening. He's caught in the frenzy. 'Your honour! Please may I bring forward a witness?' Pierre Etchebaster, distracted momentarily, looks down towards me, nods, then bangs his gavel-racket on the bench. The noise diminishes. The stranger comes around the net post and takes the witness seat.

I am not sure how to start. 'Who are you?' I ask.

'My name is Professor Doctor Eugen Herrigel,' he announces with a German accent. 'In the 1930s I spent six years in Japan studying archery with a Zen master.'

'And what did you learn?' I query.

'One of the most significant features in the practice of archery, and in fact in all the arts as they are practised in Japan, is that they are not intended for utilitarian purposes only or for purely aesthetic enjoyments, but are meant to train the mind; indeed, to bring it into contact with the ultimate reality. Archery is, therefore, not practised solely for hitting the target; the swordsman does not wield the sword just for the sake of outdoing his opponent; the dancer does not dance just to perform certain rhythmical movements of the body. The mind has first to be attuned to the Unconscious.'

The quiet voice floats over the net, hypnotising the spectators into silence. The judge, his eyebrows raised, is looking perplexed. Then he speaks: 'Excuse me Monsieur, Monsieur . . . '

'Herrigel. Professor Doctor Eugen Herrigel,' says the archer.

'Monsieur Herrigel, tennis, as far as I am concerned, is not a matter of the "unconscious". It is a matter of technique. I have written a small treatise on tennis in which I describe, for instance, the technique required to execute eight different serves. But never once did I see any need to mention "ultimate reality".'[108]

The archer continues: 'If one really wishes to be the master of an art, technical knowledge of it is not enough. One has to transcend technique so that the art becomes an "artless art" growing out of the Unconscious. In the case of archery, the hitter and the hit are no longer two opposing objects, but are one reality. The archer ceases to be conscious of himself as the one who is engaged in hitting the bull's-eye which confronts him. The aim consists in hitting a spiritual goal, so that fundamentally the marksman aims at himself and may even succeed in hitting himself. Archery is the contest of the archer with himself. So it should be with tennis. When you aim for the grille, aim for your inner self.'

Wayne jumps up: 'What is this hocus pocus! To win the point you've got to blast the ball at the grille as hard as you can so your opponent can't cut it off with a volley.'

Unperturbed by this outburst, the archer resumes, his words rippling gently around the court. 'I found my training difficult. My ambition to succeed was at first overwhelming, especially when I discovered that I found it hard even to draw the bow. Over time I became less interested in my success, and drawing the bow and releasing the arrow became less strained, and eventually artless. I learned that there is one scarcely avoidable danger that lies ahead of the pupil on his road to mastery. Not the danger of wasting himself in idle self-gratification — for the East has no aptitude for this cult of the ego — but rather the danger of getting stuck in his achievement, which is confirmed by his success and magnified by his renown. In other words, of behaving as if the artistic existence were a form of life that bore witness to its own validity.'[109]

The archer pauses, then rises to his feet while smoothly drawing an arrow from the quiver and placing it in the bow. He stands still with the bow drawn for long, long seconds, eyes closed. Then he releases, and the arrow flies in a beautiful slow arc across the net, over the heads of the spectators, and into the winning gallery at the hazard end of the court, where it strikes the brass bell hanging in the netting. The archer remains still while the concentric circles of sound gradually fill the court. When the ringing disappears into nothingness he walks slowly back to the net post and through the opening out of the court, into the darkness.

Nobody moves. The judge looks around the court, then turns towards the jurors. 'I believe we now have sufficient evidence to judge this case. Jurors, what is your verdict?' The jurors huddle together, there is a brief murmuring and they resume their places. One of them, a bearded Victorian gentleman with almond eyes, stands up. It is Julian Marshall, author of *The Annals of Tennis*. 'Your Honour,' he says. 'I have always believed tennis to be the king of games and the game of kings, a sport demanding an usual degree of skill, activity and endurance.[110] I myself have been a most passionate and ambitious player. Oh, how well I remember the sweetness of victory when I won the Silver Racket competition of 1867 . . . But something about today's strange events has changed me. Never has a tennis court been witness to such unusual happenings as we have seen here. I now realise that our beloved game can become something more than I had ever imagined, if each of us pursues it in the appropriate fashion. It certainly requires passion and dedication, as the prosecution makes clear. But if we are to elevate tennis into an artless art we cannot allow ourselves to be overcome by personal ambition and achievement, by the desire to succeed at the expense of others.'

'Give me a break!' cries out Wayne.

'Silence! Please continue, Mr Marshall' Pierre responds.

'The members of the jury have come to a decision,' announces Julian severely. 'With respect to the crime of insufficient passion, it is obvious that the accused is not guilty. Regarding the crime of lacking ambition as a player, this is a more complex matter. The defendant does indeed appear to be in want of the drive and desire to develop his potential as a player. There is no excuse for not training harder and getting fitter. He has the speed and grace of an elephant.' Julian Marshall looks expectantly towards the crowd, some of whom acknowledge his paltry jest with faint laughter, before continuing. 'And yet . . . the jury now understands why he has minimal interest in winning or losing. When he plays a match, he

Julian Marshall, esteemed member of the jury.[III]

is playing himself as much as his opponent, and we find this peculiar trait most admirable. We thus find the accused Not Guilty of lacking ambition as a player. But we declare him Guilty of the lesser crime of sloth, for which the punishment will be a regular course of running, swimming and gymnastic exercises for the remainder of his playing career.'

The judge bangs his gavel-racket on the bench and cries out, 'Case closed!' Julian immediately comes across and pats me on the back: 'Congratulations, young man'. Wayne then approaches with outstretched hand: 'No offence buddy – I just wanted to make sure you got off your lazy ass.' I shake his hand weakly, exhausted but enjoying the feeling of relief at the verdict. Pierre now comes down from behind the bench towards us. 'Well, gentlemen,' he says, 'a fair result, I would say. Now, let's clear these fools out of here and play a little doubles, no?'

4 Serving to Gentlemen

In *Down and Out in Paris and London*, George Orwell describes his months employed as a 'plongeur' or kitchen-hand in an expensive Parisian hotel in the early 1930s. Eton-educated Orwell and the other scullions laboured in the dark cellars eleven hours a day, often seven days a week, and for abysmal pay. They were forced to do their menial tasks for the wealthy guests at a furious and exhausting pace, walking back and forth around fifteen miles a day. Orwell concluded that 'a plongeur is a slave, and a wasted slave, doing stupid and largely unnecessary work . . . educated people, who should be on his side, acquiesce in the process, because they know nothing about him'.[112]

More recently, Zadie Smith's novel *White Teeth* features a middle-aged Bangladeshi working as a waiter in an Indian restaurant, whose customers barely look up at him as he takes their orders. He dreams of recovering his dignity by wearing a placard around his neck that proclaims to the world: 'I am not a waiter. I have been a student, a scientist, a soldier, my wife is called Alsana, we live in East London but we would like to move North. I am a Muslim but Allah has forsaken me or I have forsaken Allah, I'm not sure. I have a friend – Archie – and others. I am forty-nine but women still turn in the street. Sometimes.'[113]

All day every day people are serving us: waiters in restaurants, cashiers in supermarkets, tellers in banks, customer service agents in distant telephone call centres, cleaners in our homes, plumbers, accountants, bus drivers, road builders, personal trainers, sewerage workers. How much do we really know about their work and personal lives? If we knew more about who they are as people, would we treat them as we do?

SERVING TO GENTLEMEN

Our local postman might be a published poet, an expert on genetics or a dedicated volunteer at a local hospice, but how often have we invited him in for breakfast and a chat?

The great unspoken shame of our society is that the millions of people in service professions are largely ignored by their customers, clients and beneficiaries.

The world of tennis has service at its core. Each tennis club usually employs two or three professional players who, on behalf of the members, string rackets, make and sew balls, give lessons, clean courts, organise games and tournaments, and umpire matches. It was only after playing for more than ten years that I realised I had made little effort to discover how tennis pros really felt about their work. I had never seriously attempted to see the world from their perspective. Did they feel like a Parisian plongeur or a Bangladeshi waiter – overworked, underpaid and largely ignored? Were they little more than modern-day slaves, utterly dependent on the club for their livelihoods and constantly doffing their caps to the members?

My conversations with tennis pros revealed that few today feel treated like servants. Most see themselves as managers in the leisure industry rather than glorified butlers. The majority love their work and feel respected by the club members for their talents as players and coaches. The members are frequently friends as well as 'customers'.

Some of the older pros I spoke with, however, had vivid memories of the days of 'gentlemen and players'. This was a period lasting until around the late 1970s, when club pros were generally treated as servile inferiors by their amateur members. Here you will meet two professional tennis players from this older generation. Their work on behalf of club members provides universal insights into how those who serve others – whether in tennis courts or elsewhere – understand what they do, and how those who are served might act differently in the future.

*

I walked through the door of a bungalow in a village outside Cambridge and was immediately offered a glass of Frascati. It was 10 am. I declined while my host poured himself a drink and lit a cigarette. My plan to speak with a sober Brian Church by arriving early in the day had failed. Yet even under the influence of alcohol, Brian, head professional at the tennis court in Cambridge for 38 years until 1996, had an astonishingly good memory and sharp mind and wit. As we talked, my limited vision of him as a talented athlete who drank away his potential began to fade.

Brian died in 2002, not long after my visit. He was one of the great characters of English tennis, best known for his fondness of following – or replacing – a lesson with a glass of 'hubbly bubbly' or a visit to the pub at the end of the road. He was also infamous for his gambling and chauvinism, and much loved – usually by male players – for his filthy jokes, (often tall) stories and camaraderie. Brian was proud of his record as a coach, having taught former World Champion Howard Angus, and older players remember him as a beautiful exponent of the cut floor shot.

He was born in 1933 in Willesden, north-west London, where his father was a hairdresser. After leaving school Brian worked as a newspaper copyboy before being recruited as a promising young cricketer to the ground staff at Lords (home of the Marylebone Cricket Club or MCC), along with other talented working class boys. While receiving some cricket coaching, the boys were effectively treated as 'slave labour,' according to Brian, spending most of their time painting the stands and doing other menial jobs. Few of them were destined to make a living as cricket professionals.

The MCC is famous for being traditional and elitist: its all-male membership policy ended only a few years ago. It is less well known for its tennis court, which is nestled in behind the cricket stands. Until the 1970s, the majority of English tennis professionals received their initial training as an Assistant to

Brian Church in the late 1970s.[114]

the Head Professional at the MCC. Brian was one of them. In the early 1950s he left the cricket staff and took up a vacancy as an Assistant at the tennis court, where there were better prospects of a steady income and long-term employment.

※

In the film *Chariots of Fire*, based on a true story about runners striving to compete in the Paris Olympics of 1924, there is a moment when one athlete, Lord Lindsay, voluntarily gives up his prospects of winning a second medal by allowing another man to run for Britain in his place. Lord Lindsay, educated at Eton and Cambridge, represents the Victorian ideal of the gentleman amateur. He runs for the love of his country, not for money. He embodies values such as fair play, loyalty and courage. He is willing to sacrifice individual glory for the good of his compatriot. For more than a century this ideology of amateurism has pervaded Britain's elite public schools and universities.[115]

When Brian became a tennis professional, the upper class members at the MCC undoubtedly identified with these amateur ideals (as many of them still do). But did the belief in 'fair play' in sporting contests extend to the way that the members treated the tennis professionals? What was life for the professionals really like in the years after the Second World War?

Brian's main functions were to make balls, mark (umpire) matches, string rackets, and wait upon the members. There was little opportunity to work on improving his own game. The pay and conditions were appalling. Up to one-quarter of his wage was based on tips. He and the other professionals were given no extra payment for providing lessons, were expected to call the members 'Sir', and were not permitted to change in the same room as amateur players. These practices still exist at Lords.

Brian recollected how 'you used to have to go in and run the members' baths for them, test the temperature with your elbow, fold up their socks and pants, and wait on them as a valet would do, and then you used to hope that they would leave you sixpence on the tray in the room'. As a mere Assistant there was no guarantee that the tip would be his: 'the problem was that Jack Groom [the Head Professional] always found something for you to do before the member left the dressing room and, of course, Jack whipped in there and got the sixpence! He was one of the meanest people that I've ever come across in my life. If there was a hundred per cent going at the court, he took ninety-nine per cent and the other pros shared out the other one per cent between them. In those days there wasn't a marking fee, so you can guess who did all the marking. He ruled with an iron fist and everyone else starved.'

SERVING TO GENTLEMEN

According to Brian, one of his fellow assistants, Henry Johns, hung on at Lords uncomplaining, waiting to become Head Professional himself. Henry, unsurprisingly, continued the traditions of his predecessor. In effect the pros were trapped in a system of divide and rule, scrabbling amongst themselves for a few coins tossed towards them by the wealthy and often titled members.

The real problem, Brian told me, was not the other professionals but the club members, the 'gentlemen amateurs'. Amongst his earliest memories is the first ever match he umpired, when in his late teens, between an army major and a colonel. 'They knocked up, and in those days the pro used to say, 'Are you ready, sir? Time'. And I was standing with my toes out of the marker's box. The colonel came over, and he looked down at my toes, and got his racquet and he thumped it on the floor, missing my toes by about that much, and he broke his racquet! Any rate, that didn't worry him, you know. So he said, 'That will teach you to keep your fucking toes in, Church'. And that was my introduction to umpiring. And obviously I was a nervous wreck, I made so many mistakes.'

The amateur players at Lords constantly reminded the pros of their inferior social status: 'They were a pretty awful lot [back in the 1950s],' recalled Brian. 'In fact, I cannot remember ... I'm hard pushed to remember one member who wasn't ... well, instilled in class consciousness. You couldn't imagine, possibly, the class consciousness there was in those days. I will give you a perfect example. Jack Groom was very keen on boxing and the old Lord Aberdare had a box at the Albert Hall. And he invited Jack Groom, on his birthday, to come along and watch the boxing, and then they would have dinner at Lord Aberdare's house. And Jack went, thoroughly enjoyed the boxing, went to Lord Aberdare's house, and the butler came in and called that dinner was served. Jack got up to go into dinner, and Lord Aberdare said, 'Oh, Groom, you're eating round here', and Groom went in and had dinner with the servants.

The old Lord Aberdare, remembered for his backhanded comment, 'Oh, Groom, you're eating round here'.[116]

And I could tell you so many instances of that, but they just used to treat you as shit, quite frankly. This was in the days of gentlemen and players.'

The distinction between 'gentlemen' and 'players' was the dark side of the amateur ideal so revered by the English upper class. 'Fair play' only extended to those of equal social standing. The gentlemen needed somebody to score the matches, string the rackets and run the baths. Of course, certain acts of kindness towards the pros were occasionally permitted and desirable, but you would never want them to dine with you or marry your daughter.

Walk into one of England's older tennis courts today and you can see the remnants of this distinction between gentlemen and players up on the walls. In the fading photographs from the early twentieth century, the amateurs tend to be sitting in chairs or standing up while the pros are frequently crouching in front of them or sitting cross-legged like children in a primary school photo. Even more striking is the

In this photograph from the re-opening of the court at Petworth House in 1959, two Lords professionals, David Cull and Henry Johns, sit at the feet of the English upper class. The three central figures standing behind them are Lord and Lady Egremont, and Lord Aberdare (whose father sent Jack Groom to eat with the servants).[117]

way players are named in the older photos and paintings: the pros are usually identified by their full names but the amateur players are treated in a more dignified manner, being referred to as 'Mr,' followed by their initials. These antiquated naming practices were common throughout tennis clubs until only a decade or two ago.

✻

'It is not a figure of speech, it is a mere statement of fact to say that a French cook will spit in the soup – that is, if he is not going to drink it himself.' So observed George Orwell in the Paris hotel where he worked. I am reminded of a plumber who told me that if he isn't offered a cup of tea by his customer, when he finishes the job he might tell them that they can't use the shower for five days until the adhesive dries – even though it would be perfectly dry the next day.

Such everyday forms of resistance, however small or indirect, help those who are treated as servants to defy authority and retain their self-respect without overturning the system itself. For decades tennis pros have, on occasions, used equivalent subtle methods of resistance. Their strategies include telling a demanding member there are no courts available for them to book when there may well be, doing poor stringing jobs that require constant repair, and giving close calls against them when marking their matches.

Brian Church, when at Lords, took this resistance a step further than the majority of tennis professionals: 'There was one chap I disliked more than most, and his name was the Most Reverend Arthur Buxton. He ran Lincoln's Inn Fields and was a member of the Buxton's brewing family – they owned all the pubs in the North – and he never gave you a farthing. Never. When he came off court, you used to go over to the tavern and have to get him a bun and a pot of tea, on a tray. I had no option. Whatever he used to say, I had to do. However, I was offered the job at Cambridge, so I was leaving the MCC, and as far as the Most Reverend, I couldn't give a fuck! Any rate, he came off the court, and it was pouring with rain, I mean sheet rain, and he said, "Oh, Church", he says, "My bun and tea", and I said, "It's pouring with rain, sir", and he said, "Oh, a drop of rain won't hurt you". So I went over to the tavern, got his bun, soaked it in a puddle, and poured all the tea out of the pot and filled it up with rainwater, by which time he was in his bath, and you had to serve him tea, and hand it to him in the bath. And I poured out his cup of tea and he took this cup of rainwater, and he said, "As usual, Church, fantastic!" He went up slightly in my estimation after that! Incredible! Although some people were terrible to me, it didn't worry me. I just used to think, "You're stupid." '

✽

Brian started as the Head Professional in Cambridge in 1958, 'on terrible money and with terrible accommodation'. He initially earned £8 a week and received 1/6d professional fee for giving lessons. He was also given a 'shambolic' house attached to the court: 'The ceiling had holes, the slats were missing, there was an outside toilet and no bath bar a tin bath'. The court itself was 'indescribable . . . there were cobwebs from top to bottom and no one had cleaned it for 18 months'. He set to fixing the house before his wife arrived. He also cleaned and painted the club.

While some members at Lords were addicted to tea and buns, Brian soon discovered that the young upper class gents at Cambridge University were unusually fond of tea and cake: 'When I'd been there about six weeks, and my wife came down with the new baby – and we didn't have any money whatsoever, and when I say 'whatsoever', we didn't have a half a crown, you know – we bought a chocolate cake as a treat. This was on a Saturday afternoon, I shall never forget it. There was a knock on the door and there were two Old Etonians stood on the doorstep, and they said, 'Oh, we are thinking of taking up real tennis, how do we go about it?' 'Come in, gentlemen', you know. Anyway, they came in, they had tea, and we offered them a piece of chocolate cake, and they ate the lot! So we didn't have any cake, which we'd been looking forward to! They went out, and Peggy said, 'I do feel sorry for those boys. They're obviously starving'. And I said, 'Peggy, your first lesson. Never feel sorry for an Old Etonian'.'

Cake was not Brian's only hardship. His workload increased since he was running the Cambridge court on his own rather than the work being shared between three pros as had occurred at Lords. Moreover, he was still treated with disrespect by club members: 'I had to cover 50 balls a week. I was by myself. I used to play for 1/6d, about six hours a day. I used to have to repair rackets. In those days it wasn't like it is now, it wasn't remunerative at all, because you charged three pence a string, and the undergraduate didn't pay you in any case! So

THE FIRST BEAUTIFUL GAME

it was a total disaster, you know. You used to work incredibly long hours. When there was a match on, I used to have to light the fire in the dressing room, the coal fire in the dedans, go on court at 11 o'clock to start marking the matches, serve them lunch (which my wife used to get), go on court at 2 o'clock. And then a great chap, ———, who is now Lord ———, used to say, at about four o'clock, 'Brian, would you like a break for ten minutes? You'll get the tea, won't you'. And you used to have to – that was my break. It was quite extraordinary! Pros nowadays, they obviously wouldn't stand for it. But we didn't know any different, which was sad.'

*

As I listened to Brian speak, glass in hand, speech beginning to slur, I wondered whether professionals during his era could have shown stronger resistance to the upper class members. Why did they allow themselves to be trampled on so easily? Brian, for example, continued calling the members 'Sir,' just as he had done at Lords. Why didn't he simply start calling them 'Mr,' as a first step to using their first names? Why didn't he demand better wages and conditions?

In some ways the lack of resistance is unsurprising. Brian was living in an age when the class distinctions and social hierarchies of Victorian England were still pervasive. The idea that one should serve and obey one's superiors was reinforced by education, politics, the press and religion. Punch cartoons poked fun at the stupidity of the poor while clergymen quoted biblical passages that legitimised the class system: 'Servants, be obedient to them that are your masters according to the flesh, with fear and trembling, in singleness of your heart, as unto Christ' (Ephesians vi. 5,6).[118]

Apart from the general force of class ideology, there are several other reasons why Brian was so accepting of his subordinate position. One is that everyday forms of resistance allowed pros like Brian to maintain a sense of dignity and self-respect. George Orwell's experience suggests a second explanation: he describes how the cooks in the Paris hotel did not look upon themselves as servants but as skilled workmen or artists. On this basis the cook 'despises the whole non-cooking staff, and makes it a point of honour to insult everyone below the head waiter'.[116] In other words, the cook survives servitude by envisioning a hierarchy that extends below him and treating those beneath him as inferiors. Although the cook recognises that he is subordinate to the hotel owner and customers, he still sees himself as a kind of a lord, with the plongeurs having the role of slaves.

Like the Parisian cooks, Brian ensured that there were people he could look down upon: 'I have to say that, to a degree, I encouraged this stupid snobbishness, because I called the members "Sir", and when I eventually got an assistant, I insisted that the assistants called me "Mr Church", which didn't go down very well. All my assistants, previous to the last one, called me "Mr Church". And I thought, "Well, if they didn't, I had no discipline whatsoever", you know, "No good them coming in and calling me 'Brian' ". You may see that or may not. I know it's entirely different now. All my assistants, I treated them very well, and they all respect me – or I'd like to think they do. I don't know whether you've met any that don't, but to my face, they all respect me.'

What Brian doesn't say is that his assistants were not only required to call him 'Mr Church' but were also made to do most of the hard work, such as making the balls and cleaning the court. Former World Champion Wayne Davies told me that he has, over the years, encountered several examples of this kind of power relationship between head professionals and their assistants: 'It's like an animal house, like battered children becoming battering parents'. In his experience, 'if a committee browbeats the head pro, then the head pro's going to do that to his assistants'. Hierarchy and authority will, like genes, reproduce themselves.

George Orwell observed not only the cooks but also the waiters: 'His work gives him the mentality, not of a workman, but of a snob. He lives perpetually in sight of rich people, stands at their tables, listens to their conversations, sucks up to them with smiles and discreet little jokes. He has the pleasure of spending money by proxy . . . The result is that . . . the waiter comes to identify himself to some extent with his employers. He will take pains to serve a meal in style, because he feels that he is participating in the meal himself.'[120]

Brian Church's little jokes were far from discreet. But like the waiters – and unlike most tennis pros of his era – part of him desired to participate in the social world of his clients and become one of them. Over the years this developed into a deferential attitude towards Old Etonians and other members of the upper class that became a third reason why he accepted his servitude. He liked showing off his acquaintance with aristocrats or the fact that he had taught Prince Edward and Prince Charles to play tennis. One of his favourite stories of this kind concerns the Duke of Roxburghe, with whom he became 'quite friendly' when an undergraduate at Magdalene College. One day after the Duke had played with his (then) brother-in-law, the Duke of Westminster, Brian invited them out for a drink at his local working men's club. The two aristocrats were wearing scruffy clothes and trainers. All three were having a drink at the bar when one of the committee members came in: 'Roger comes over to the bar, and he said, 'Brian, you haven't signed in your guests'. 'Sorry, Roger, I'll do that in a moment'. So he comes up a bit later, and he said, 'Brian', he said, 'I know you think you're God Almighty, but you're like every other person here, you sign in your guests'. 'Sorry, Roger'. So I go over, sign in the Duke of Westminster and the Duke of Roxburghe. Roger ambles over to the book, has a look in there, he comes up to the bar, and he said, 'Brian', he said, 'I'm fed up with you, you're always fucking around!' I think that's a classic.'

SERVING TO GENTLEMEN

In Victorian and Edwardian England, servants in the great country houses often considered themselves to be the aristocracy of domestic service. According to one study, they 'basked in the reflected glory of their high born employers.'[121] Brian shared this attitude. His view of society also reflected that of his members. He was a confirmed royalist and described himself as a 'staunch Conservative'. He told me: 'Labour are against most things that I agree with, they're for most things that I don't agree with. I don't agree with all this welfare and benefits and things like that. I think that a person should stand by themselves. If they need help, they should get it. But the help has to be proved. I will go down to a pub in the village, and they're living in council houses, they're getting rebates, they don't pay council tax, and I think . . . "I'm paying it", and it just annoys me.'

I often think of Brian as a kind of outspoken and untamed version of the butler Crichton in J. M. Barrie's Edwardian comedy play *The Admirable Crichton*. Crichton is a Conservative who privately disapproves of his master, Lord Loam, having Radical political views and finds him 'not sufficiently contemptuous of his inferiors'. When Lord Loam declares that class divisions are artificial, Crichton replies: 'The division into classes, my lord, are not artificial. They are the natural outcome of a civilised society. There must always be master and servants in all civilised communities . . . for it is natural, and whatever is natural is right.'[122]

*

Brian's drinking, stories and wild antics made him a favourite with many Cambridge undergraduates. Several became his friends and regularly visited him in later years. Yet his behaviour was not always appreciated. His wife, Peggy, left him for a time, but later returned. 'I've had a great time, I have to admit — I've met so many people. But I was stupid, I put the club before my wife, quite frankly, because I loved the situation.

With hindsight, I'd never do it again.' Despite the long hours Brian spent at the club, most members eventually came to consider him a liability. They felt his drinking, chauvinism and unreliability deterred people from playing and created an unsavoury atmosphere in the club. In the mid-1990s they effectively ousted Brian from his job.

When I spoke with Brian, he and Peggy were no longer living in the house attached to the tennis court but in a housing development in a village near Cambridge. Brian, now retired, seemed to have nothing to do but drink himself to death. He was bitter about the way the committee had treated him after almost forty years of service and furious that the new Head Professional was given a much better pay deal than he had ever had. After a few drinks Brian told me how he had hoped to supplement his meagre pension with funds raised at a retirement dinner to be attended by the wealthy amateur players who he considered his 'friends':

When you left Cambridge, did they give you a kind of retirement fund?

'Yes. Not through Cambridge, but there was a dinner at the MCC, and people, not mainly from Cambridge . . . haven't got it here, but I can show you a list of all the people that gave, and I got £11,000.'

Lovely! That's really nice!

'£11,000 divided by 38 is fuck all. That's an insult.'

I sat there, silent. Some cigarette ash fell down Brian's shirt as he took another sip of wine. The tiny room was filled with smoke and a sense of total betrayal.

✽

Kevin Sheldon, Head Professional at the Leamington Tennis Court Club, is the opposite of the boisterous and reckless Brian Church. Under thick brows, his eyes are soft and kind. He comes across as mild-mannered, thoughtful and humorous. People consider him the gentle giant of the tennis world. Kevin frequently expresses concern about his financial security. 'I'm a habitual worrier,' is one of the first things he told me. He is also extremely modest. Now in his early 50s, he is still admired for his beautiful stroke-play. 'I don't like blowing my own trumpet,' he said. 'I'm not a great one for letting everyone else know what a great player I am, or was, and who I've beaten'.

Kevin had originally planned to study business management at Lanchester Polytechnic when he left grammar school. Then, through his old headmaster, he heard about the job as real tennis professional at the Leamington Tennis Court Club. He was already playing the local lawn tennis circuit and thought that it was a chance to play 'the real thing' – lawn tennis at a serious level. That was until he looked up real tennis in the Pears Encyclopedia. His father, who died soon after and was a shop steward at a nearby Coventry car factory, seemed happy with Kevin's new plan. But his mother wanted him to do a proper job with more security, like working in a bank.

I asked Kevin what working conditions were like when he started his new job: 'Awful. When I first came here in '68, I remember, for a lesson, I'd get £1 an hour. That's not that long ago, and they were . . . they were very . . . I won't say mean, that's probably the wrong word, but very careful, and they didn't want to spend too much of their money on me. Now I'm self-employed but at that stage I had a retainer, and then I'd get fee money. Obviously, I had the shop. But, yes, it was . . . being a single man, I suppose, and fairly naïve, I suspect that I didn't kick up too much of a fuss at the time.' At least, unlike many other professionals at the time, Kevin received some payment for giving lessons and could make a little extra money stringing and selling rackets.

Like Brian Church, Kevin seemed to accept his subservient position through youthful innocence and naïvety. When he arrived at the club he felt 'slightly overawed' because 'there were some quite important people here' such as owners of

Kevin Sheldon on his home court at Leamington.[123]

Coventry City Football Club. Kevin was originally 'quite nervous' and cautious in his relations with the members. One member began calling him 'Ken' by mistake and continued to do so because Kevin lacked the boldness to correct him. The club atmosphere used to be very formal: 'You could offend if you were slightly over-friendly, you had to watch your Ps and Qs much more than I think you do now.'

How did Leamington compare with other elite clubs such as MCC in London? 'There was no touching your forelock, or 'Sir' or 'Let me put your shower on for you'. Yet after a few months Kevin began to realise 'that it was a sort of out-of-town MCC,' especially with respect to its all-male policy and the way members treated the professionals. 'It was a bit us-and-themish, a bit gentlemen and players. Some of the older members here really felt that the pros should be . . . not dirt, but they should be a servant, they should be like a steward or a butler, just be a servant of the club. They didn't think that they should have any standing, and that certainly applied in the late sixties when I started.'

One of the tasks Kevin shared with professionals at MCC was scoring friendly games between club members: 'When I first came here, every match was marked. God Almighty, I'd forgotten about that! I remember . . . if you had ten hours a day, bloody hell! Any Tom, Dick or Harry would have to be marked. I can see, now, why, because what they were doing was supplementing my income – in other words, getting the members to pay me. So instead of paying me a higher retainer, and not marking, they'd pay a lower retainer so I'd have to mark to get the money. I could see what was happening, now. And, for the three or four years I was here when I first started, that was the case. But then, as the fees went up, people decided not to have a marker. I suppose, now, I find marking, to be honest, easy money. If I've got some balls to do, I'll sit at the back with five balls and mark. If I was doing five balls anywhere else, I couldn't do it any quicker, and I've earned myself some money into the bargain, and you can give a little critique afterwards, of how you thought the players were playing. Sometimes people feel marking's slightly demeaning, but I don't find any problem with it, maybe because it comes quite easily to me.'

For the amateurs, having their game marked was simply considered part of the service, similar to the way that pros were expected to sweep the courts and sew the balls. The members did not want the pleasures of playing to be hindered by having to remember the score or bend down to pick up a tennis ball. Their tennis was to be like a sumptuous meal where there were servants to cook the food, serve it, pour the wine and clear up afterwards. All they had to do was indulge themselves. As Kevin came to realise, the best way for the members to ensure such service was the unsubtle method of paying him such a poor basic wage that he was forced to score games to earn extra income.

A book about the club, written by one of its members, discusses the case of another of the professionals, Chris Ennis, who took over from Kevin for a short time in the mid-1970s. Ennis seemed to show more resistance than his predecessor. After failing to have his pay and conditions improved after winning the British Open in 1975, Ennis resigned, writing what the author describes as 'a somewhat insolent letter to the club chairman, larded with references to feudalism and forelock tugging'. The author notes, with some distaste, how Ennis's attitude was 'far from the typical professional of the "old school"' and that he was one of a 'new breed' of professionals who 'did not expect to be asked to mark friendly matches between members and wanted higher payments for coaching them'.[124]

Working at Leamington also had implications for a professional's wife. Kevin told me how his wife, Jenny, felt when invited to special club functions in the 1960s and 1970s: 'She used to come a fair amount to start with. I think she found some of the wives quite difficult . . . because the blokes who came here had quite a bit of money . . . and the wives sometimes . . . I wouldn't say she felt inferior, because she's not inferior at all, but she felt that they had a fair amount of dosh, and she hadn't. It's very difficult to explain, but for a woman, I think she felt slightly out of place, and she tended not to come. That's changed a lot over the 30 years.' Throughout the country, especially before the 1980s, it was common for tennis pros and their wives to be snubbed at club events or not to be invited at all. At many clubs it was also expected that the pro's wife would cook lunch for inter-club matches on weekends, usually for free and with little acknowledgement. Some wives of professionals, such as Lesley Ronaldson and Viv Dawes, also sewed balls and strung rackets – again without due recognition or remuneration. Although Leamington has changed, it remains a man's world that, according to Kevin, is still 'fairly intimidating for the girls'.

If you were a tennis professional at Leamington in the 1970s or 1980s and wanted to influence how the club was run and improve your working conditions, would you be able to? The answer is almost certainly 'no'. This was not only because the professionals then had no right to sit on the club committee. Many club members told me that it was because the club was effectively ruled as an autocracy — sometimes benign, sometimes not — under the chairmanship of one of the members, John Camkin. According to Kevin: 'Whenever there was a Committee Meeting, you'd have an agenda, and everybody would be sitting round, and then Camkin would come in. He was a very large personality, and he was a very persuasive man. He'd come in, and he'd say, 'Right. This is what we're going to do on that topic. And that's what we're going to do there'. And everybody said, 'Right, okay, that's fine,' and then they'd all troop out again!' I asked Kevin whether this system worked for his own benefit: 'Well, it did, if what he wanted was what I wanted. But if what he wanted wasn't what I wanted, then that was just too bad. If he liked you, and he liked most everybody, then that was fine. But if he had it in for you — he never had it in for me — one of the pros, he didn't like him at all, and he was a bit nasty to him . . . not nasty, but wasn't helpful. When Camkin left it became much more democratic.' The rule of John Camkin was not typical of every tennis club in England but it highlighted the dependence of club professionals on a 'gentleman's' committee over which they had little control.

*

While the tennis pro offered services to the members, some members offered their own services in return. Several pros I spoke with recalled how if they had a sports injury or a tax problem, there would be a doctor or an accountant who played at the club who was ready and willing to help, often at a moment's notice and without cost. In Kevin's case, the club did not provide accommodation for the professional (unlike at other clubs such as Cambridge) but there were well-connected club members prepared to assist him: 'Through various contacts at the club – estate agents and people who were in building – I managed to get into a little semi-detached house, and then to a bigger house, and then a slightly bigger house. This probably sounds absolutely disgusting to you, but they'd got a plot that was going, you know, and somebody just cancelled. "Would you want it?" This was when I was still in the flat, and I went along, and there was nothing, it was just a big slab of concrete on the floor. So I said, "Well, where is it, then?" And it was the late seventies when houses were being snapped up, and he said, "We haven't built it yet, but if you don't want it . . . in ten minutes back at the office I can sell it to somebody else". I said, "Oh, go on then, I'll take it".'

Kevin appeared slightly embarrassed at this privileged treatment he received from club members. But to me it seems, at the very least, a fair exchange given his poor wages and working conditions during his early years as a pro. This kind of reciprocity was (and still is) an essential element in the relationship between amateurs and professionals. Until the status of club professionals improved after the 1970s, it was part of the system that sustained the hierarchical relationship between gentlemen and players. A little generosity from the members compensated for the servitude and gave pros a sense that they were respected.

※

As we sat talking upstairs in the still and timeless atmosphere of the members' dining room, I asked Kevin the main question that I had been pondering as he spoke: why had he stayed working at Leamington for so many years?: 'Yes, I thought that might be coming!' He had obviously been asked the question before. This is not surprising because over the years he has been offered jobs at other clubs in England and Australia but has never taken them. He told me how, in 1973, he felt that tennis was not giving him sufficient financial security, so he went to work in a bank in Coventry for a few years. He liked the regular hours but didn't like being deskbound. 'I was sitting down all day, and I just hated that — I just want to be active, I need to be up and doing things'. He also found that 'they'd give you a good bollocking if you made a slight mistake'. Kevin decided to return to the tennis club, feeling it was now a career for life.

His return was partly dictated by his love for the game, 'As you know,' he said, 'you get hooked.' But there was a stronger force acting upon him: 'It's appalling to say this, isn't it . . . I don't think I'm a terribly ambitious sort of person. I'd worked here for a while, enjoying it a lot, and we'd got two young children who had just started school. I think, possibly just for them, I wanted a bit of continuity, and Jenny was quite settled here as well, and all our family was round here . . . I'm sure I could possibly have bettered my situation by moving maybe, but the club seemed quite happy with what I was doing, and I was quite happy. I felt the members were very appreciative of what I was doing. It's not a tangible thing.' Kevin spoke about his lack of ambition as if it were a character flaw. Perhaps he regretted not taking the opportunity to work as a professional in Australia and not pushing himself harder to become one of the finest players of his era, which undoubtedly he could have been.

Kevin was searching for respect as well as security and stability. Although sometimes treated like a servant during his early years at Leamington, he gradually began to feel that the members were 'very appreciative of what I was doing'. Now, after thirty years at the club, Kevin told me: 'They treat me with a deal of respect, which I'm quite pleased about. If I was unhappy here, if I felt that they were just treating me like a bit of dirt, I would go. But they don't. I feel that I'm valued.' This respect manifests itself in many ways. He is now fully self-employed and free to generate income from the court rather than relying on a retainer from the club. He also has a seat on the tennis committee. Moreover, he now calls most of the members – some of whom he considers friends – by their first names: 'In fact, if I call somebody "Mr So and So" they think I'm taking the mickey half the time!' The club, he said, is no longer 'run by a small elite, a wealthy little clique'. The members are 'just ordinary chaps who pay their subscriptions, come along, play tennis and go – there are no pretensions at all.'

Although many outside observers still consider Leamington an elite and chauvinistic gentlemen's dining and drinking club, Kevin genuinely feels the atmosphere has mellowed. He had recently spoken to a long-standing member, who he has known since the late sixties: 'He said, 'Kevin, the club seems to have lost a little bit of its style.' And I thought, 'Well, that's probably a good thing, we're obviously doing something right then'.

*

The stories that Brian and Kevin told me about their pasts are an important record of how individuals have negotiated and survived everyday relations in the English class system. I have also found their experiences a source of inspiration in my own life: they have made me become more conscious of how I treat those people who provide me with services and sustain my lifestyle, whether it be tennis professionals or others. I am now more aware that they might feel ignored or unappreciated by customers and clients. I make a greater effort to look the supermarket cashier in the eye as I say thanks when she hands me my change. I talk to my accountant about how his work affects his personal life. I ask waiters about their passions and aspirations, and their thoughts on politics and art. I want to respect all these people as individual human beings, not treat them as impersonal 'service providers'.

I believe that discrimination, inequality and injustice are often a product of our inability and unwillingness to see the world from the perspective of other people. Talking to them about their lives is one way of creating empathy. But it is not enough. A deep understanding of others' lives and predicaments must be based on experiencing what they experience. This is why I began to explore what daily life was like for the tennis pros at the club where I played. I asked the Head Professional to teach me how to sew a tennis ball. I thought it would be easy to stitch the felt cover onto the ball and that while doing so, I'd be free to let my mind wander and think about articles I might write or new recipes I could invent. But I found sewing tennis balls a frustrating experience that required considerable concentration to do well. And I was unable to contemplate articles or recipes while I focused on ensuring the consistency and spacing of my stitches. Moreover, I soon became bored with the task. Until then I had never fully appreciated how mundane the daily activities of a tennis pro can be. One small result of my experience is that, unlike many other amateur players, I rarely complain to pros about the quality of the balls on court.

Another result is that I now feel a moral obligation to experience what working life is like for other people whose services I desire or require. I recently had some builders do an extension on the kitchen. Although they made the main structure, I took part by mixing cement, laying the floor tiles and building the kitchen units. Once you have done some of this hard physical work you will never again complain about your builders punctuating the day with multiple tea breaks. They are needed to recover energy and concentration. You will also be less likely to consider the initial quote to be overpriced, since you will appreciate that building work is highly skilled and demanding.

Tennis has taught me that empathy is a product of listening to others and sharing their experiences.

5 *The Missionary*

'I suppose I've just always had a missionary sense about tennis,' he told me. 'It was my thing I was going to do.' Chris Ronaldson has been a tennis professional for over thirty years and is perhaps the most famous living player in the world. He no longer has the shoulder-length dark hair and moustache that gave him a slightly satanic look when he first began playing. Now in his early fifties, he is tall, slim and strong. His words are few and considered, his face impassive. He might intimidate you a little. But his eyes are playful, his wit acerbic, his feelings strong.

Chris is renowned not only as a player, having been World Champion for most of the 1980s. He has also played a major role in transforming tennis from an obscure pastime for the upper class into an expanding and exciting sport that now receives some television coverage. He is as close as tennis gets to having an equivalent of the nineteenth century cricketer W. G. Grace, who popularised the sport to such an extent that it became a defining aspect of the Victorian age and an enduring symbol of Englishness.[125]

To revive and transfigure a game that had been in decline for over two centuries, Chris approached tennis with the dedication of a missionary and the vision of a revolutionary.

Chris has done three things that most of us do not have the courage or will to do. He has actively challenged social injustice: in his case, the subservient position of tennis professionals that was common at most clubs until the 1970s. He has pursued his great passion with absolute and unwavering commitment. And he has defied the social convention of separating our work from our personal lives and passions; every aspect of

Chris Ronaldson in the late 1970s, and (right) *marking from the dedans at Hampton Court Palace in 2006.*[126]

his life has been absorbed into tennis – his family, his friendships, his leisure time, his privacy, his intellect.

The result is an extraordinary life. In his own words: 'Tennis has given me everything I wanted – my job, my wife, my lifestyle. This is a game which has taken me round the world. I couldn't want for anything more. I certainly wouldn't want to be involved in anything else. You read that 90 per cent of people in this country are dissatisfied with their job . . . I'm one of the ten per cent that isn't.'

The story of Chris Ronaldson is not only the story of how tennis has changed beyond recognition but the story of how we can all discover a different way of living.

✼

I spoke with Chris in his living room, an apartment attached to the tennis court at Hampton Court Palace just south of London, where he has been Head Professional since 1979.

Lesley Ronaldson[127]

Over the years he has been a professional at courts throughout the world, including Melbourne, Bordeaux and Troon in Scotland. But his life in tennis began in Oxford in 1971.

After failing his degree at the University of Kent in Canterbury, Chris hoped to become a lawn tennis coach. In the meantime he found a job on a building site. Before long a friend pointed out an advertisement for an assistant at the Oxford University Tennis Club. Chris realised that this meant real tennis not lawn tennis but 'because it offered the chance to learn to string rackets and because anything was better than standing around a freezing construction site in winter, clutching a rule and counting down the minutes to the next tea-break, I decided to give it a go'.[128] Within an hour of arriving at the court he had been accepted for the job.

He quickly fell in love with tennis but could also see that the game was dying: 'I think the mentality that existed in the early seventies was, 'We have to keep this old game going,' and people played, such as they did, out of duty. All the courts were damp and dark, and people paid the minimum possible,

50 pence or something for a game and, therefore, it wasn't possible to have clean courts and club rooms and bright lights. The atmosphere was definitely one of survival. The game was very restricted, in those days, to Army and Public School, and I'm afraid to say that those two particular groups held the game back enormously, and almost caused its death. If this game had remained in the domain of the Old Public School Boys, it would have done.'

While Chris aimed to become the finest player in the world, he also wanted to revive tennis. He recognised that doing so would require completely devoting his life to the sport. Together with his wife Lesley, who later became British Ladies Open Singles Champion (1979–86) and a professional player, he worked to expand the popularity of tennis beyond the narrow confines of the British upper class, to increase the number of women players and juniors, to bring old courts back into use and to build new ones, to develop the tournament circuit, to encourage respect for the professionals and to improve their working conditions: 'I was one of the first pros, of the new generation, who thought about it as not just a job, but as a way of life, and who wasn't prepared to sit back and watch the game go downhill.'

Making tennis a way of life is exactly what he did. All his time, energy, relationships and thoughts were channelled into tennis. Lesley was just as devoted to the divine calling of tennis as her husband. She told me about their early days in Oxford, when they were first married. 'As soon as Chris took up the job he fell in love with the game. He got completely hooked on it and I did too.' Up a narrow stairway next to the court was the professional's work area and behind that another tiny room: 'Chris used to sleep in there, he actually had a mattress there, in the room. You see, this is his dedication. We bought a little house but didn't used to go home. We used to get woken up by the knock of the first person on the court, so he'd get up. I used to go back to the house sometimes but then strung rackets all night to make money. And of course you had matches and the only day he had off was Sunday and we just basically collapsed because we worked all day and all night, every day of the week. It was complete dedication.' Stringing rackets and scoring matches were not the only tasks: 'We sewed balls all day long,' recalled Lesley. 'In those days we sewed them on trains, we sewed them on buses. We always seemed to be sewing tennis balls.'

Being an amateur at the time, Lesley couldn't earn money for all the work she did; she was effectively an unpaid professional. But her work made an important contribution to Chris's earnings. It also meant she could spend time with her husband: 'I don't think I'd have seen much of Chris if I hadn't, and that's why I've always been so involved.'

Since their time in Oxford, Chris and Lesley, together with their three sons, have always lived 'on site' in a flat or house attached to the tennis courts where Chris was the professional. While most pros who live at their courts keep the door between club and home firmly closed when the work day is over, the Ronaldsons have never taken this approach. There is little separation between the family's private space and the members' areas of the club. This is obvious from a visit to their apartment at Hampton Court. They share their kitchen and telephone number with the club. 'We were phoned at half past ten last night, someone wanting to book a court for next week!' said Lesley, smiling but a little exasperated. Members occasionally wander into the family dining room during dinner parties. There always seems to be some pro from one country or another staying the night, especially if there's a tournament on: the house is full of spare mattresses. Most of the Ronaldsons' friends are tennis players or have been converted into tennis players. And Chris, in particular, never stops thinking about the game. When we spoke he had just returned from a walking trip in Tanzania, taking some club members up Kilimanjaro. While there, he said, 'I was dreaming up ways of

THE MISSIONARY

getting balls made in Africa.' Work and life are fully integrated. As Chris put it: 'It's all intermeshed, it's all one lifestyle. It's our life!'

Tennis has become a family affair for the Ronaldsons. Lesley eventually became a professional player in 1988, so she could be paid for her work at Hampton Court (having until then retained her amateur status as there were more tournaments she could enter as an amateur). She also runs a company promoting corporate tennis events and tournaments, and has played an important role in the administration of the game, being a founder of the Ladies Real Tennis Association. Two of their three sons became tennis professionals. Their eldest son, Ivan, is now Head Professional at the Washington court, having turned pro in 1994. Their middle son, Ben, works as an Assistant Professional with his parents at Hampton Court, living in another apartment at the opposite end of the tennis court. Chris's brother, Steve, became a professional player, as did Steve's son, Matthew. Chris's father, until his death in 2004, ran a small company that publishes books about the game (including this one); Chris's sister is now involved in the business. The Ronaldsons have become a tennis dynasty, resembling the Tompkins family who were tennis professionals generation after generation between 1758 and 1930, mostly at the court in Oxford.[128]

I asked Ben, who was born in 1976, what it was like to grow up completely immersed in the world of tennis: 'This has been my life, the Palace. Part of the job is that the home phone is the real tennis phone. Whenever the phone goes, you don't know if it's going to be a friend or a member, or both. Because I grew up with that, this is standard for me. I just don't have a problem with it. But people always talk about how they'd hate my father's job or, at least, if they had his job, they'd change it. They'd get a new phone line upstairs, they'd work specific hours, and once you reached ten o'clock, that's it, not answering the downstairs phone any more. And Dad can't

Ben Ronaldson.[129]

bring himself to do that, he always wants to know what's going on. We're used to seeing people walking in and out as if it's their living room. So I was brought up, basically, in a family, a huge family, which is all the members. That's the way it was. I'm very comfortable with the way it is now. I don't really feel like I want to change anything.'

Lesley considers their lifestyle a matter of choice: 'It's our decision, the club doesn't force it upon us'. If they weren't prepared to pick up the phone at any time or string a racket late at night, 'then the service wouldn't be there'. I asked Lesley if she ever felt the lack of privacy: 'Yes, a couple of years just after Luke [their youngest son] was born. That was because I was down and it just got on top of me a bit. But we've always lived in very happy chaos, with people coming in and out, nobody knocks, the doors are open. It's a happy house. If anyone asks us if they could stay the night, Chris and I, we'd never so no, ever. No one uses our bed, though – one rule!'

✢

After over a quarter of a century as the Head Professional at Hampton Court, Chris is treated with enormous respect by the club members and by the tennis world in general. He earns a good salary and is able to run the club freely, without being treated as a subservient employee by the club committee. He helps finance the re-opening of old courts and development of new ones. He is famous as a former World Champion, as a coach, and for his teaching manual 'Tennis – A Cut Above The Rest', which is also available as a video. For years he was a central figure in the Tennis & Rackets Association (T&RA), the ruling body of the game that is primarily controlled by amateur players, and he plays an important role in the International Real Tennis Professionals Association (IRTPA). His opinion is sought on virtually every major decision in the game, from new tournament rules to the materials required for building a new court. The man who was once a missionary has become a god.

But when Chris began as a professional in the early 1970s it would have been almost impossible for him to envisage such a future. He told me about the appalling position of tennis pros at that time, particularly at clubs like Lords (MCC) in London. 'In those days there was very much a class divide,' he recollected. The pros were 'functionaries, they did as they were told and didn't have any use for neurons!' Just as Brian Church described life as a pro at Lords, Chris said that being dependent on tips from wealthy members produced 'an ignominious lifestyle' for the pros, who 'used to hang around and tried to be on duty when the high rollers came in.'

The old attitudes were also present at his own club in Oxford: 'There were a few incidents which made me very uncomfortable. Being on the court as a marker, on one particular occasion . . . I was performing my job. One of the members took it upon himself to say that I was wrong. And he was slightly inebriated anyway, and it wasn't a question of whether I was right or wrong, it was just . . . the fact that because an amateur had said it, therefore it must be so. And you would get an incident like that, at Oxford, once every three or four months, which made you uncomfortable. But I suspected, at Manchester or Lords, it happened a great deal of the time.'

So how exactly did Chris intend to erode the feudal subservience of the tennis pro and revive a dying sport? How could he transform the game that had become his all-consuming passion?

Unlike some of the older generation of professionals, Chris was unwilling to tolerate the lack of respect for club pros. Perhaps because of his education and middle class background, which differed from pros such as Brian Church who had working class roots, he saw no reason why club professionals and amateurs should not treat each other as equals: 'I suppose I felt a bit awkward about the fact that my Senior Pro, Peter Dawes, aged 30, was calling 19 year old students "Sir". It didn't make any sense to me, having just come from university myself. I was revolutionary in that I wouldn't call the members "Sir", I would only call them "Mr. So and So".'

Even if Chris began treating members on more equal terms there was no guarantee that this would be reciprocated. It would take time to alter the attitudes that accompanied the old system of master and servant. He remembered an incident involving one of the top amateur players soon before leaving to become a professional at the court in Melbourne in the mid-1970s: 'I was just about to go to Australia, I'd been a pro for two years. Before I went, I was going to play one last British Open, as a young ambitious pro, aged 23, and —— agreed to play me in a friendly game. I wasn't employed, I was between jobs. So I just phoned him up and said, "I've got a couple of courts booked, would you play me?" And we had a couple of hours. I can't remember who won, but he was certainly better than me. We went up to the bar afterwards, where a couple of his friends were. He'd offered to buy me a drink. As I came in, very ostentatiously he said, "Oh, by the way, Chris, thank you ever so much", and gave me a 50p . . . and I looked at it, and said, "No, no, that's all right". "Oh no, I insist!" and it was such an ostentatious thing really. And I suppose that had quite an effect on me. I thought that was wrong. I'd invited him . . . if he'd have rung me up and dug me out of bed in the middle of the night, or arranged for me to come down from Oxford to play a game, and given me a tip, especially if he'd done it quietly in the corridor afterwards, then I think I probably would have accepted it, at that stage, in the spirit in which it was intended. But it seemed to be . . . it may not have been . . . but it seemed to be a very public putdown. "You're a professional, I'm inviting you into the bar here to have a drink with me, but don't forget who you are," and I didn't like it.'

According to Chris, this amateur player has now changed and would probably be embarrassed by his past behaviour. Such traditional attitudes and practices have been largely expunged from the tennis world. But refusing to call the members 'sir' was not going to be enough to transfigure the game.

*

Together with a few other professionals and some dedicated amateurs, Chris helped instigate a series of innovations that have revolutionised tennis. Primary amongst them was the way that professionals were paid.

In the old days most professionals received a flat rate of pay. No matter how many lessons they gave, rackets they strung or matches they arranged on behalf of their members, they still received the same low wage. This is the system that older pros like Brian Church were reared in. Chris was at the forefront of encouraging club committees to introduce more incentives into the wage system. In addition to receiving a basic retainer, the pros would take a cut of their lesson fees and the court bookings, and would also earn money from stringing rackets, and selling rackets, shoes and other sports items. In his first job at Oxford, in the early 1970s, Chris was paid £8 a week. The earnings of a Head Professional today are usually between £25,000 and £35,000. A few top pros are able to earn more.

The improved incentive pay structure, which quickly spread throughout the country, helped revitalise the game. The pros now had a reason to get more people playing, for the more courts they booked, the higher their earnings. Before the changes, courts such as Hampton Court would sometimes have had only a few hours play a day, and even fewer in the summer low season. But once Chris arrived in 1979 and had an incentive to book up the courts (and was willing, with Lesley, to put in the time), court usage increased to over 12 hours a day, year round, and soon reached over 5,000 court hours per year.[130] The same story was repeated at other courts and by other pros. It now became standard for pros to spend much of their time on the phone, ringing around their members to arrange games for them.

The higher earnings potential for tennis pros had another consequence, which was to attract a better educated and more ambitious workforce. According to professional Peter Dawes, from the 1970s the game started to have 'some more intelligent professionals who had different backgrounds, different attitudes to what they saw as their role.' This included not only Chris Ronaldson, but people such as Mick Dean and Alan Oliver, who had both worked as town planners and had degrees from Cambridge and Oxford respectively. Both left their careers to become tennis professionals, recognising that the improved pay levels and working conditions meant they could earn a reasonable living while doing something they loved. Club members and committees were suddenly faced with a professional who they could no longer treat as some uneducated inferior. The new generation of pros not only commanded more respect but were often far more ambitious than their predecessors. They wanted to broaden the membership base, they wanted to expand the tournament circuit and increase prize money through attracting new sponsors, they wanted to see new courts built.

The building of new courts has been an extraordinary change in the game. The court built in 1986 at the Oratory School near Reading was the first new court constructed in the UK for almost a century. In subsequent years other new courts have opened in Bristol, Essex, and in Chelsea Harbour and Hendon in London. Previously abandoned courts have been brought back into play, for instance in Dorset, Newmarket and Cambridge. In 1975 there were around ten active courts in play and 13 professionals. Today there are some 26 courts in play in the country, requiring over 70 professionals to run them.

The expansion has partly occurred because tennis has benefited from the growing popularity of 'alternative sports' (such as martial arts and mountain biking) amongst Britain's middle classes since the 1980s. It is also due to professionals like Chris Ronaldson proving that tennis was neither too difficult nor too strange to become popular and that it was possible for a good pro to fill up a court from morning until night, making tennis clubs a viable financial venture for the funders. Some pros have even become owners themselves. Chris is part-owner of the court at Holyport, near Maidenhead; on Hayling Island, Peter Dawes eventually became a director and shareholder of the Seacourt club. These professionals are reviving a tradition common in pre-revolutionary France, when the *Maître Paumier* owned and ran the court himself. While building a court remains expensive (around £400,000), pros such as Chris have ambitions to create a national tennis centre with multiple courts.

Unlike 30 years ago, club professionals are now able to earn moderate amounts of extra money doing what they are good at, which is playing tennis. Chris, together with other pros such as Lachie Deuchar and Lesley Ronaldson, have played a central role in attracting new sponsors into the game, boosting tournament prize money. In 2004 Rob Fahey received $57,400 for winning the World Championship (a result he repeated in 2006), with the runner-up, Tim Chisolm, earning $16,500. A top professional can expect to earn around £200 in appearance money for playing in a Premier Division match in Britain's National League. Such sums, however, are miniscule compared with the rewards for highly-ranked lawn tennis professionals and golfers. The result is that almost every professional must maintain a job as a club pro to survive financially.

In addition to improving conditions for the pros, and helping to develop innovations such as the computerised handicap system (see Chapter 3), Chris realised that it was vital to dispel the traditional image of tennis as an elite game played by former Public School Boys: 'It needed to be packaged differently. It needed to be presented as something like . . . 'This is the best game in the world, and we have the best pros in the world, and you can go and play squash if you like if you want to be a cheapskate, but why not play something you're going to really enjoy? And it doesn't cost that much, anyway.' There were no ladies playing in 1970, maybe one or two worldwide, and they were sort of . . . oddballs! It's ridiculous to think, now, but I remember, we used to say this game is too difficult for ladies, the equipment was something ladies couldn't handle. Absolute rot! And it's just been repackaged to include ladies and juniors, as something exciting and progressive.'

While Chris and Lesley Ronaldson led the way in recruiting a broader spectrum of members, much of the repackaging has been taken on by the International Real Tennis Professionals Association (IRTPA), founded in 1975, and the Ladies Real Tennis Association (LRTA), founded in 1981. In recent years the IRTPA – which acts as a kind of trade union – has become increasingly active in pressuring for decent conditions for club professionals, obtaining greater media coverage for the sport and promoting its expansion amongst young players and women. There is now a growing circuit of junior and women's tournaments, and a smaller proportion of players from England's upper class.

Several other professionals have also played an important part in changing the image of the game and the membership profile of the typical tennis club. Amongst them is Kees Ludekens, Head Professional at the court in Cambridge and one of a contingent of Australian professionals working in England who have helped introduce a more egalitarian ethos into tennis: 'Ten thousand flyers go out every time we run a course, so really any punter who can afford to play can come and play real tennis here. If you look at other clubs, and Oxford's an example of that, you have a much greater proportion of ex-Public School boys. With them comes, I think, the perception that a real tennis pro should be the person who makes the balls, cleans the court, much more of the traditional Lords professional. A lot of the members at Cambridge are an exception because of the way I've done my recruitment. In the past it was all Lords here, it was men, it was Public School boys, you had to be a certain person to be invited.' Walk into the club room at Cambridge today and you are more likely to find the owner of a local curry house having just come off court than an Old Etonian in a knitted cricket sweater.

Parallel to Chris's impact on the wages and working conditions of tennis pros, has been his influence on their status and sense of self-respect. Kevin Sheldon, the Leamington Head Professional, made this clear: 'I'm earning now what I didn't think I could possibly be earning ten years ago. This is partly to do with Chris. He's raised the status of the pros . . . and he's shown tennis clubs that they've got to pay for the pro, it's not something that can be taken for granted, or just treated like a chattel. They've got a valuable resource and it's got to be paid for. If you want a pro to give you a lesson, if you want to use the tennis court, you've got to pay for it. And I think that's filtered through everywhere, and long may it continue. He's done a lot for the pros. You might find some amateurs saying he's not done very much for the game, but certainly, for us, he's done a lot. He was really instrumental in dragging the pros up by their bootlaces and giving them a lot more standing in the tennis community.'

Kevin told me, however, that the old subservient position of the tennis pro still exists at a few clubs: 'Without Chris we'd still be in dark ages of David Cull, Henry Johns [former pros at Lords in London], running the members' baths and touching your forelock, which is just not on . . . calling everybody 'Sir'. The Lords pros still do it. Absolutely astonishing! When I was at Lords recently, I said to Chris [Swallow, Assistant Professional], 'how are the finances and everything going?' He said, 'Well, it's all right'. And I said, 'What do you get paid for marking?' 'We get paid blah-di-blah'. 'What do you get paid for a lesson?' 'Nothing.' I couldn't believe it! I said, 'What?' He said, 'No, the club take the money'. I says, 'You are joking!' It's just a throwback, isn't it, to the Dickensian age. It really is.'

Despite all the changes, life remains a struggle for Assistant Professionals, and not only those at Lords. In addition to being burdened with most of the menial tasks, such as sewing balls, assistants can earn as little as £12,000 per year, and a trainee even less. Lachie Deuchar, British Open champion from 1986 to 1991, was clear that their pay and conditions remain intolerable: 'How many people could be an Assistant Pro at any club and be able to afford to get married and have kids? Ask yourself that basic sort of question. How many clubs have got a pension plan in place for their Assistant Pro? And then you ask yourself how morally responsible those administrators are. Just ask the question! If people do respect you they will pay you, and the fact that they don't pay you means they don't respect you. Clearly. QED. The pros need to get hold of

THE MISSIONARY

the purse strings to change that.' One consolation is that the current situation is better than in 1978, when Jonathan Howell had to pay out of his own pocket for the training to become the professional at the Moreton Morrell tennis court in Warwickshire. As he laments in his memoirs, 'Unthinkable today, but at the time we knew no better'.[131]

Chris Ronaldson, missionary and quiet revolutionary, has been the major force in helping the pros know better.

*

There is no change without resistance. For three decades Chris and other progressive tennis professionals have struggled against a hard core of amateurs, particularly within the Tennis & Rackets Association (T&RA), who have resisted the innovations he has encouraged. The tension between the two sides, more often expressed in polite verbal exchanges than overt conflict, has a meaning beyond tennis. It represents a clash between England's old feudal order and a modern, egalitarian society.

The T&RA, the sport's governing body, was founded in 1907. According to some players, it remains dominated by a male fraternity of public school-educated amateurs. Like the House of Lords and fox hunting, it has been described (perhaps unfairly) as a social anachronism, a cul de sac where England's dwindling upper class has been taking refuge while society changes around them. Until recently the T&RA's Chief Executive was a retired Brigadier and there are still a number of aristocrats within its councils and committees. The game of rackets, which is even more obscure than tennis, is only played at a small number of elite public schools such as Eton and Harrow.

In 1990 the lawn tennis magazine *Tennis*, which for a short time contained a few pages each month on real tennis, carried an article that seemed to encapsulate the attitude of the amateur traditionalists within the T&RA towards the growing status and demands of professionals:

View from the Dedans by Reg Majore
'Real tennis is one of the last remaining bastions of amateur sport; a magnificent game rippling with tradition and the Corinthian spirit.

As such it behoves us all to protect it from the vicissitudes of an age in which sport is associated with drugs, commercial abuse and hooliganism, rather than honour, dignity and athleticism.

The most damaging of all the evil modern influences is professionalism and immediate action is required to prevent this parasitical menace from assuming control.

Real tennis professionals are in place to attend to the production of balls, effect the maintenance of courts and rackets, and provide coaching and marking services. It is not part of their function to attempt administration of the game, nor to determine policy, yet somehow the professionals have managed to pervade all levels of the Tennis and Rackets Association in order to promulgate their narrow and self-serving, minority views. The most recent example of this shameless self-aggrandisement is the deplorable issue of muddled professional views on marking.

The T&RA must act now to restore the tennis world to rights and to remind professionals that the interests of the paying majority must prevail over those of the greedy few.'[132]

This extraordinary article, echoing the language and attitudes of Victorian amateurism, provoked a highly emotional response in the letters pages in the following issue. One player from the all-male Leamington club wrote the following: 'Hooray! At last someone is prepared to put into print what the majority of real tennis players have been talking about in private over the last few years. Of course Reg Majore is right in what he says about "the parasitical menace of professionalism".'

THE MISSIONARY

This response was atypical. Most amateur players were in total opposition to the views of Reg Majore. One stressed: 'I have yet to meet any of the real tennis pros you are describing. The ones I know are hardworking, honest individuals who are devoted to the game.' Another amateur, who had played a central role in building new courts, said that the 'patrician attitudes of Reg Majore will do little, if anything, to enhance the game'. He emphasised that some of the greatest contributions to tennis have come from leading professionals such as Chris Ronaldson, who frequently give their advice and help without any expectation of monetary award. His letter ended with a rejection of Victorian amateurism: 'The old ways and days of Gentlemen vs. Players are over. Nowadays we are all players'.

There were also measured responses from two professionals. Lachie Deuchar felt that the author of such 'potentially offensive views' should not hide behind a pen name. Chairman of the Real Tennis Professionals Association, Peter Dawes, wrote that Reg Majore's views were not in the best interests of the game and suggested that his column be withdrawn. This is exactly what happened. Reg Majore's column never appeared again.

I have sometimes encountered old school types with views similar to this 'Reg Majore', although they are usually the kind of people I try to avoid. For many of them tennis is not just a game, it's a status symbol, and if too many people play then its elite status is diminished. Tennis is a world of order and tradition in which they feel comfortable and protected from the clamour of modernity. They don't want money and media to intrude. They want the professional to be on call to restring their racket or sweep the court. And they don't wish to lose the regular Saturday morning court that they've had for twenty years to some junior or woman player. These are the kinds of people who inhabit clubs such as Lords, Leamington and Manchester – although not all the members share such attitudes.

THE FIRST BEAUTIFUL GAME

So who was Reg Majore? Was he a typical club member and proof that tennis was still dominated by an amateur elite? Or was he, as was more likely, a dinosaur from the old days, one of those public school-educated traditionalists who still lurked in the corners of some clubs and sat on committees of the T&RA? The answer is neither. Many years later the truth became known. It was Chris Ronaldson.

Chris was intent on caricaturing some of the old guard because he believed they were preventing the development of the game. He told me that while there are some progressive amateurs in the T&RA there are others 'who feel very threatened by the direction that some of the professionals are taking'. The latter worry that the game is expanding too rapidly and fear that it may become like lawn tennis, in which a huge influx of money effectively destroyed the game's ethos and traditions.

Chris gave me an example to illustrate his point. 'I can tell you a story, of ten years ago, about when we set our targets for the nineties in 1990. Our target was to build three to five courts in this decade. There was a member of the T&RA who said, 'Three to five courts? Let's be reasonable about this. Let's say we only build three courts. Do you realise that means that we might have to have 300 new members, 300 new people playing this game? Where are we going to get them from?' And he was serious. He thought that there weren't 300 worthy people in this country left to play this game, and it's that type of attitude we've got to get rid of. And this was a person who really deeply and passionately cared about the game and where it was going. But that type of Old School has got to be swept aside and trodden upon, and there's a lot of it left.'

While Chris was cautious about openly criticising the T&RA when we spoke, several professionals were more vociferous in their views. They admitted that the association has played an important role in the development of tennis by funding the building of new courts and the refurbishment of old ones, and helping finance the training of assistant professionals. However, they were keen to provide examples of the T&RA being 'anti-pro'. For instance, the T&RA has a reputation for trying to prevent the emergence of 'touring professionals' (that exist in many other sports such as golf) unattached to any club, sending the message that the only appropriate role for a pro is to serve his or her club members by stringing rackets, sewing balls and marking matches. Some argue that the association keeps too large a percentage of tournament sponsorship money for itself rather than making it available as prize money. According to one outspoken professional, who wished to remain anonymous: 'The T&RA lie, cheat and steal. That's my experience. This is where I get radical. I've had a lot of experience of them now, I've watched them operate and they do. What's good for them isn't good for us. But it's not like a huge cabal, it's not a 'they', it's on an individual basis.' Such strong views are not the norm.

Julian Snow was, until recently, the Chairman of the T&RA's Tennis Committee. Son of a Herefordshire solicitor, Julian was educated at Radley College and after university became a trader on the London futures exchange. In 1996 he gave up his job to become a professional gambler, specialising in horse racing. Julian has been the top-ranked amateur player in the world for around two decades and for a short time in 1992 was the number one in the world overall. He has won a record 17 British Amateur championships in a row, several British Opens and remains one of the finest players in the game, even at the age of 41.

I spoke with Julian in the quiet and comfort of the Manchester Tennis & Racket Club which, despite recently opening its doors to women members, retains the air of a Victorian gentleman's club. Julian enjoys the atmosphere of such places, describing himself, and the people who he considers his good friends — mostly middle-aged men — as 'clubbable'. He takes tennis more seriously than almost anyone I have ever met, spending months preparing for big matches and practising with absolute dedication and focus: 'I've sacrificed vast areas of my life for my tennis and I don't regret it in the least. Financial, social, career, whatever. Everything. You're only young once. That's what I say to other youngsters. You can work hard in your 40s and 50s if you really want to. There's no point in settling yourself at Goldman Sachs when you're 25. You can't get back the time when you are young and keen and fit and able to beat these people. There's no point in semi-retiring at fifty and then playing tennis every day — it's too bloody late, mate.'

Julian described his role as Chairman of the Tennis Committee at the T&RA as one of 'encouraging participation'. He expressed frustration at the lack of good young players at the top of the game: 'I think one of the downsides of tennis is, because there are so few people playing, the turnover of opponents is small. Last time I won the British Open, in 1998, which is six years ago, the seeds were Fahey, Bray, me, Gooding, Male, Wood, Virgona, and Gunn. And seven of those eight are still playing and they're still the same sort of level in the rankings. And I got bored of playing the Opens, not only because I can't win them any more, but because, what's the best that can happen? You are playing Gooding or Bray or Wood again and again and again and again. It's like bloody Groundhog Day.'

Although a man of few words, and terse at best, Julian had strong opinions on the role of professionals. I asked him what he thought about those professionals who wanted to have more influence in the administration of the game: 'Oh, I think they're all mad, those lot are mad, and the other point is that the regular pro thinks they're as mad as we do. It's unrealistic, isn't it, because it's only silly amateurs like me who are holding everything back, and if sensible forward-thinking modern professional people could control it, the whole game could expand and take off and there'd be prize money and television

*Julian Snow, off and on court.*¹³³

and courts everywhere and it's all mythical, in my view. I think they live in cloud cuckoo land.'

As Julian continued, I realised that I had never heard him speak with such animation – and at such length – in my life: 'And some idiot like ——, who's fifth in the world or whatever the hell he is, if by chance it all did take off like they think it might do and should do if they were controlling it and there were academies in Moscow, he would be two hundred in the world, not fifth in the world. And he'd still be earning the same amount of money as he is now. And he's only number five in the world because it is a tinpot game played only by about five thousand people worldwide. I don't make any great claims to fame. The idea that I could have been number one in the world for a year exemplifies the fact that it is a minor sport. It's not any the worse for that – it's the best ball game, in my view – but we must be realistic and keep a sense of proportion. Other people might think that was a very backward and negative point of view.'

145

What is the appropriate role for a professional, according to Julian? He told me he liked clubs where the professionals are 'well trained, and they're respectful without being groveling.' He particularly enjoys playing at clubs such as Manchester and Leamington because the pros 'don't want to take over the club, but they want to improve themselves and earn a decent wage.' A good club pro should be providing an exemplary service to the members: 'That's what members like. I like someone who holds open the door and says, 'Yes sir, no sir, thank you sir, and well played,' and all this sort of stuff, and is not chippy. That sounds old-fashioned and borderline snobbish, but it's still true.' Why do you like those things? I asked him. 'Because it makes life easier, and you feel better for it, rather than have some chippy pro who's sullen and resentful. It's the reality of life. When I'm at work, the other fella's the client, and if he says, 'Do this, do that,' you just say, 'Sure.' And it's the same here, it's not demeaning, it's just their role. It's just their job. The chippy pros are chippy because they feel that what they're doing demeans them somehow. They're better than all the members, but they have to perform a service because they're a pro. It's a job, like a fellow in a golf club. It doesn't demean anyone to give lessons, or clean the clubs, or sew balls, it's just a working environment. I find it very wearing, all these people who get uptight about things that don't actually matter.' I sensed that my questions were also becoming wearing on Julian and brought our conversation to a close.

While most club players may agree with Julian that tennis is unlikely to become a mass sport like football, few share the view that professionals should be little more than service providers for their club members, that they should, in effect, be seen but not heard. Throughout the tennis community there is enormous respect for the role that pros such as Chris Ronaldson have played, and continue to play, in revitalising and promoting tennis, just as there is enormous respect for Julian's talents on court.

THE MISSIONARY

I did, however, encounter a supporter of Julian's vision in Brian Church, the maverick professional at Cambridge for almost forty years. Brian considered himself a professional of the 'old school' and accused modern pros of being 'too commercial'. In his opinion: 'Although they were trodden on, and that type of thing, I think the older pros had more love of the game than modern pros, quite frankly. The modern pro, to me, has it very easy, which undoubtedly they do, but they are so money grasping! Really terrible. Which I, personally, don't like. I've never bothered about that type of thing, and that's why I haven't got any money! But I'm sure I had a better time than they're having now, although I had nothing.'

What do you think professionals have contributed to the game? I then asked Brian. 'I think some pros have . . . most have not. The people that have contributed to the game more than pros, are amateurs. You have to differentiate between pros in the past and pros now. What makes me laugh is, you go to a T&RA Dinner, and at the end they always say – 'Were it not for the pros, the game would fold up tomorrow'. That's a load of bollocks. If every pro resigned, in the country, amateurs would carry it on. But there's not one pro that would carry it on if he didn't get paid. I've seen this round all the clubs. I go to Newmarket a lot, and there are people there that, for the love of the game, keep it going. I think that's the same in most clubs. You'd always get one nutcase amateur who would give up all his everything for real tennis. I don't think there is a pro in the country that would give up everything for real tennis.' Brian was, of course, wrong. Professionals such as Chris Ronaldson have dedicated their lives to the game.

Chris – like many of the pros I spoke with – does not characterise the relationship between amateurs and professionals as a major clash or antagonism. He also hinted that my questions were making too much of the distinction between the two: 'There are a few pockets of people who have a downtrodden look – not most pros, but some pros have a downtrodden look – from years of abuse at the hands of their members. But there are not many like that these days. I sense that you're looking to try and create conflict. I don't think there's real conflict there.'

Perhaps he was right: there is far more cooperation than conflict between professional and amateur tennis players. Chris remains a moderate in his attitude to future change. He has a strong allegiance to the T&RA and shares, with many of the old school, a great desire to maintain the traditions of the game, such as saluting your opponent before the match begins, crossing the net in the right order, wearing white, and keeping out bad language. But he feels that these traditions can be maintained while also having 'brightly painted courts, and sponsors, and women and juniors playing the game'. The future, according to Chris, is about 'striking the balance between tradition and progress'. It is also about overcoming partisan differences and showing the world that tennis is an extraordinary sport that can be played by anyone: 'We have the opportunity now to put the game back on the map, to make a success of it. It's such a great game. The game is bigger than any club or any individual.'

What is the legacy of Chris Ronaldson? Arrive at most tennis clubs today and you will find that the Head Professional is more of a manager than anything else. He will be organising tournaments for the members and sponsorship deals, attending committee meetings, overseeing the accounts, planning strategies to increase the number of young and female players, or raising funds for a new glass wall at the service end of the court to improve viewing. He might also be giving a lesson, but is unlikely to spend much time sewing balls or stringing a racket, tasks that will be mainly left to his assistant. He, like his assistant, will call the members by their first name, and vice versa. He will be good friends with some of his members and may occasionally play golf with a couple of

*Unlike photos from earlier times, today's professionals no longer sit at the feet of lords and ladies.*¹³⁴

them. Despite being a professional athlete, he will still spend most of his time running the club rather than training for matches and playing tournaments. The 'he' may even be a 'she' – there are increasing numbers of female professionals. Only at a few clubs, such as Lords, will the old social roles of professional and amateur be played out: the pros might still call the members 'Sir' or 'Mr', they will be excluded from committee meetings and the members will be acquaintances rather than close friends. 'At Lords, they're still servants,' said Lesley Ronaldson. 'We're here to look after the members but not to pull the forelock any more.'

For decades the English upper class have remained hidden and protected within the confines of tennis. But as the game has expanded, they have been increasingly exposed to change. The old comforts they enjoyed are disappearing or already gone: the pro running them a bath; the sense of security in knowing that their fellow members attended the same exclusive school and share the same politics; their treatment of tennis courts as gentlemen's clubs. The age of 'Gentlemen and Players' is past. The tennis world, so long a stronghold of the English social elite, is no longer a haven. They must find other places to live out their slow death. Perhaps without knowing it, Chris Ronaldson has helped to extinguish one of the last remnants of feudal England.

*

Should we dedicate our lives to pursuing our passions? Should we merge work and personal life so completely that the distinction dissolves? These are the questions I think about when reflecting on the experiences of Chris Ronaldson.

Although Chris has devoted his life to tennis, he is no puritan. At one point in his career, for instance, he worked in London for four months as a futures trader: 'In 1989, I went to the City for a while to try and learn a new trade because I was worried about my capacity to earn enough to pay the school fees, in this job. I found out what it was like to be part of the rat race, which has given me a very good comparison. Two things happened. First of all I realised the benefit of working with people who were honest and bright and cheerful, which you do get in a real tennis club, as opposed to the liars and cheats I came across in the City. And secondly, my middle son got a scholarship, which took away the need for me to work there, so I very quickly got out of it.'

Chris has also sought stimulation in other fields, especially since retiring from competitive play in 1993, aged 41. 'As someone who's achievement-oriented, when I finally realised that my legs weren't going to carry me around the court effectively any more, and needing challenges in my life, I decided to rectify a blemish by getting a degree. So I signed up for the Open University in 1993, and I spent five years getting a degree. I spent the first two years doing economics, because I wanted to be able to talk to my eldest son who was doing economics.

And I also did maths for two years, which I had failed at 'A' level. But then my youngest son, who is good at maths, got too good for me. I then decided to do something for myself, so I did two years of history. Twentieth century European history is my real passion. I finished up with a B.Ed., with first class honours, of which I'm very proud.' Chris has taught history one evening a week in a local adult education college, while still doing his job as Head Professional at Hampton Court Palace. He also enjoys solo walking holidays and has climbed Kilimanjaro three times.

So even the ultimate devotee of tennis has other passions, seeks new stimulation and appreciates the benefits of having a variety of working experiences — if only to help confirm earlier choices.

Nevertheless, I still consider Chris to be a missionary. The meaning of his life cannot be separated from his devotion to tennis. And he continues spreading the gospel. The best place to hear the gospel according to Chris Ronaldson is on a tennis court during a lesson. He is acknowledged as one of the finest teachers of the game in the world. I've had two lessons from him in my life, both of which I remember with an unusual, even unsettling clarity. He began the second one hitting me a basket of balls down the centre of the court. He watched me with absolute concentration, not even bothering to hit back the balls I returned, even when they were within arm's reach. I could feel his gaze upon me. After the fifty or so balls in the basket were finished he approached the net and gave me three astonishing insights into what was wrong with my play and what I could do about it. When the hour was over, the lesson continued in the professionals' workshop, with Chris intent on ensuring I had understood his advice. I'm still practising some of what he told me in the lessons, the first of which was over fifteen years ago.

I am certain that Chris approaches each lesson with the same sense of sacred dedication and thoughtfulness, no matter

St John The Evangelist *by El Greco, and Chris Ronaldson, both with ball in hand.*[135]

the standard of the player. He is like El Greco's St John The Evangelist, tall and thin, a face of calm and quiet, but emanating intensity, passion and wisdom, and a desire to spread the word.

6 *Adventures with my Father*

I told my father that I was writing a book about tennis and that I needed his help.
— Sure kiddo. What can I do?
— Well, I want to teach you how to play and then write about the experience, I replied.
— Teach *me* to play? You must be joking! What the hell for?

I paused a moment. In the years since Dad retired I've often suggested that he does something new, such as taking up furniture making, doing some charity work or returning to the music studies he abandoned as a young man. But he always claims to be too busy, that his schedule is already full of golf, chess, visits to his brother, repairing the house. I often feel frustrated that he is unwilling to embark on new adventures. I don't understand what he's scared of. While I try not to be pushy and respect his right to make his own decisions about his life, there remains part of me that wants to inspire him with some novel passion. That's why, when he came over from Sydney with my step-mother, Anna, to visit me in Oxford, I decided to teach him how to play tennis. I wasn't intent on him becoming a tennis addict. I simply wanted to encourage him to follow untrodden paths. I thought it unwise to reveal my full intentions so concocted a more innocent explanation for requesting that he become my student.
— The thing is, Dad, that I need to let the readers know what it's actually like to play the game. So far they've read all about the lives of tennis professionals, the history of the sport and what it can teach you about the art of living. But I haven't really conveyed to them the thrill of stepping onto a

court for the first time and learning how to hit a ball.

– 'Experience is my mistress,' said Leonardo Da Vinci. Your readers aren't going to understand tennis by just reading about you giving me lessons. They have to experience the game for themselves, Dad countered.

– You're right. So was Leonardo. But reading about it is the next best thing.

– You've also forgotten that I'm too bloody old to learn a new sport, I'm 73! And I already play golf once a week.

– You can play golf any time. Try something new. The Sydney tennis court is only a quarter of an hour from where you live, I retorted.

– I don't have time, you know. There are always lots of things to fix around the house.

– Come on, Dad. Have a go. For me. Just for an hour.

– OK, mate. If you think it will help your book. But you're not allowed to make me run too much. And can I retire after the first lesson if I want?

– Don't worry Dad, you can do whatever you like.

*

I'd booked a court for eleven o'clock on a Sunday morning. We arrived early, Dad wearing an old pair of white shorts and shirt that I'd lent him. He looked out of proportion, spindly legs supporting a slightly pot belly and broad shoulders. I knew he was still quite fit but I suddenly wondered whether he could run around after a ball for an hour. How would it affect his blood pressure, which was already a little high?

– Dad, if you get tired out you can always stop before the end, you know.

– Don't worry, I'll be fine. Golf keeps me fit. And I played tennis for years, he said.

– Lawn tennis, you mean. Now you're going to play the real game you should use the correct terms. In my world normal tennis is called lawn tennis and real tennis is just called 'tennis'.

— Sorry, I forgot. You did explain it to me once. I think when Anna and I watched you play that Australian guy, Kevin, last year. You remember, the match you lost.

— His name was Kieran, not Kevin.

We were standing in the club room in Oxford, which is attached to the side of the court. I handed him a racket. He'd seen one before but now looked at it with different eyes.

— Why's it so heavy? he asked.

— Well, the ball is heavy. It looks like a normal tennis ball but it's solid. You need a sturdy racket to deal with a heavy ball that's moving fast. And a light racket, like a squash racket, would easily break under the repeated impact of the ball.

— And it really is bent! he exclaimed.

— Yeah, the racket is shaped like a hand with the fingers spread out. The asymmetric head makes the centre of the racket face actually off-centre, so you can hit balls that bounce low.

— And why don't they have graphite rackets, like in other sports?

— Graphite rackets have been banned because they'd make the game all about power and eliminate finesse. Something I love about tennis is that everyone uses basically the same model of wooden racket, which is only made by one company. So you don't get the crazy situation existing in lawn tennis or squash, where every year the racket face becomes bigger and bigger, and whoever has the most money can buy the most powerful hi-tech model. With everyone using the same racket, tennis contains a greater element of equality than many other sports.

Just behind Dad was a print on the wall, which he couldn't see. In it the eighteenth century French professional, Guillaume Barcellon, was holding a racket almost exactly like Dad, with the fingers of his left hand curled around the racket head. They both had the same muscular forearms. But while

THE FIRST BEAUTIFUL GAME

Barcellon had a sad and longing look, Dad's eyes reflected excited anticipation. As I considered these two men, I also realised that each had a son who wrote a book about tennis. Guillaume's son, Pierre, had his book published in 1800. My own was nearing completion.

Anna, who had come to watch, had been sitting quietly as Dad and I spoke.

— Don't you want to come on for a hit? I asked her.

— Ha! You know I was never taught geometry properly. All the different angles would be too much for me.

— In 1800 the great professional Pierre Barcellon, the son of the guy in the painting up there on the wall, wrote that geometricians were unlikely to be better at the game than anyone else.[137]

— Even so, he didn't know that some of us only have short legs and move like hippos.

— Another book, from the early 1900s, says that ladies should be confined to watch from the dedans seating area at the end of the court because tennis is too fatiguing and possibly dangerous for them.[138] Do you want to be like some pre-feminist Victorian woman, too feeble to play a man's game?

— You read too many books! Anyway, someone has to take the photos.

It was almost eleven o'clock, so Dad and I walked down the corridor on the side of the court and through the opening at the net onto the court itself. Dad looked around, his shoes squeaking on the worn cement floor as he swivelled. He was facing the main wall, which rose up some forty feet. Around the other three sides of the court were the sloping penthouse roofs. On Dad's right was the service end, with the wide dedans opening on the back wall and the netted galleries on the side. On his left was the receiver's or hazard end, which also had small netted openings on one side, in the last of which — the winning gallery — hung a brass bell. Dad didn't

Guillaume Barcellon in 1753.[136]

notice the bell but was looking towards the far corner of the hazard side.

— What's the red square with the horse on it?

— That's the grille. And it's a unicorn. If you hit it, you win the point. And you see that opening with the little bell? Hit that and you also win the point, I explained.

— And those lines all over the court, what are they for? he asked like a child with a thousand questions.

— That's the complicated part. They're the chase lines. Once you've learned how the chase works you can really call yourself a tennis player. I'll explain it later.

I wasn't going to confuse him before he'd hit a single ball by describing how the chase lines functioned.

— OK Dad, before we start, there are a few basic things to remember. First, always hold the racket so the head faces upwards and doesn't drop below your wrist. Second, you should maintain a firm wrist at all times. Third, you need to keep the racket swing very short. It's not like lawn tennis or squash, where you take a big swipe at the ball. Short and simple. That's all you need to know to hit a tennis ball.

Dad took a few practice swings in the air. His racket followed an arc, from high to low and then high again, like a golf swing.

— Stop, stop, stop! You have to keep the swing as short as possible. And make sure the racket head stays above the height of your wrist.

He tried again. Better. I sent Dad down to the hazard end of the court and went up to the service end carrying a basket of balls. I told him to stand in the middle of the court, a metre or so from the back wall.

— Right, I'm going to hit you some forehands to start off, I shouted down to him.

*

My father is one of the most generous people I have ever known. He has spent his life trying to help those around him. He is caring, always willing to listen to my problems and support my endeavours. He has not been consumed by ambition or the search for power, money or status. He is modest. And he can cook. I have learned from him and have tried to follow his example.

There comes a point in many parent-child relationships when the parent is no longer the teacher or authority. Instead the parent becomes the one who confides in the child, who seeks their advice and approval, who learns from them. Staring across the net at my father as he awaited the first ball felt like the moment when our relationship changed, when he became the child. I did not feel powerful or in authority. But in the unfamiliar surroundings of a tennis court I sensed his vulnerability.

Yet the idea of teaching my father anything still seemed strange. My life has been so pampered and uneventful com-

Teaching my father on the Oxford court.[139]

pared to his own. Dad was born in Poland and survived the years of the Second World War. He was then a refugee in Berlin after the war ended, suffering years of cold, hunger and dislocation. In 1951 he was finally able to flee Europe and emigrate to Australia, totally alone. As a refugee he was obliged to spend three years working wherever the Australian government sent him; he worked nights as an attendant on a tuberculosis ward in a Sydney hospital. Only then could he begin to create his own life.

What could I possibly offer a person who had lived through a war, who had begged for food, whose life experiences were so much more profound than my own?

✻

I told Dad to aim his shots for the corner of the court on my right-hand side. I hit the first ball towards him and he took a huge swipe, missing it by a foot as it skipped through below his racket head. I fed him another with the same result. The third ball hit the racket frame and dribbled towards the net before dropping into the trough where the balls collect. But the fourth ball was different. By now he had realised that a tennis ball skids quickly when it bounces on the floor, much faster and lower than a lawn tennis ball. Dad swung and hit it near the centre of the strings. The ball flew up high and onto the back wall behind me.

— Great shot! That's the way, I said.

Dad looked surprised and pleased. I continued feeding the basket of balls. Gradually he became accustomed to the pace of the ball and weight of the racket. He was still missing about half the shots but others were getting over the net, though seldom landing near the target area I had set him. More noticeable was that he seemed to be totally focused and engaged in watching and hitting the ball. Dad appeared more alive than ever, his body moving, his eyes darting.

*

After we had been on court for half an hour I called Dad to come up my end of the court. I wanted him to say that this was the most fantastic thing he had done in his life and that I had rescued him from the doldrums of retirement. But he didn't.

— Well, what do you reckon? I asked.

— I think I'm getting the hang of it. It's bloody satisfying when you hit it in the middle of the strings. The ball doesn't bounce much, though. And sometimes it doesn't bounce straight.

— You know why the bounce is inconsistent, don't you? The balls are hand-sewn by the club professionals. They're all roughly the same size and weight but everybody makes their balls slightly differently. Some are sewn very tightly and others more loosely. Sometimes the seam is quite big and sometimes not.

— Well, why don't they have manufactured balls, like in regular tennis? suggested Dad.

— Tennis players like the tradition of the hand-made ball. It's part of the history and makes the game seem more special.

I told Dad to aim his shots for the corner of the court on my right-hand side.[140]

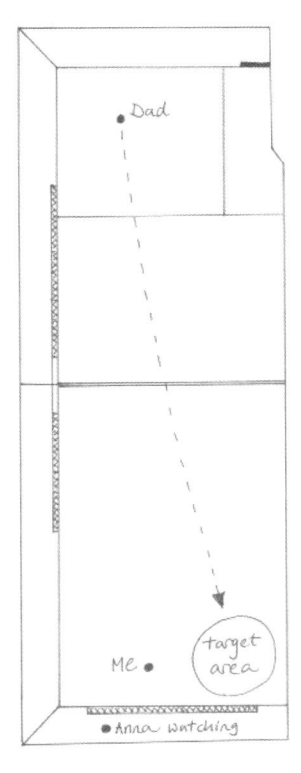

Dad nodded his head. I wondered about his attitude to tradition, and to the past in general. When playing traditional Polish folk tunes on the piano accordion his face looks serene, his eyes develop the quiet sadness that I'd noticed in the eyes of Guillaume Barcellon. I can never tell if he is just feeling the music or remembering his childhood and youth.

*

It was now time to teach Dad how to serve. We stood together at the service end of the court and I demonstrated the simple 'sidewall' serve: standing in the back left-hand corner I hit the ball gently from waist height up on to the side wall above the sloping penthouse. The ball then bounced once on the penthouse and down into the corner at the receivers end. I repeated the serve a few times so he could see what I was doing.

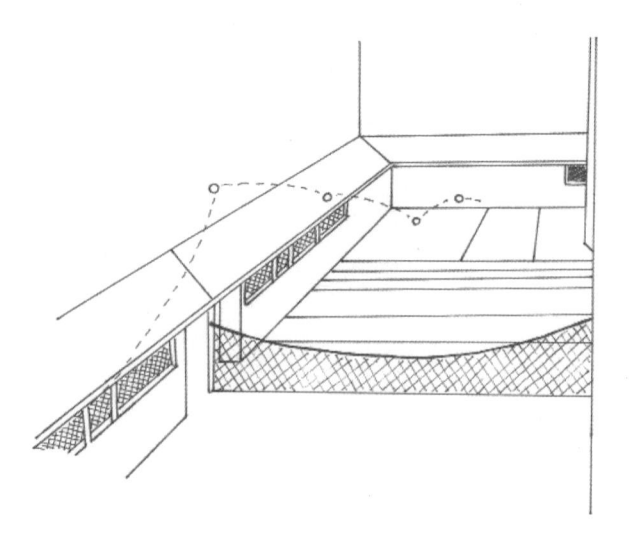

Path of the sidewall service.[141]

Dad then had a go. I watched him toss the ball in the air and swing. Far too high and hard. The ball rocketed into the side wall then ricocheted off onto the floor on the other side without touching the penthouse, making it a fault. He tried once more, but this time he aimed too low, striking the ball straight into one of the gallery openings on his own side of the court. He served a few more; they were either too high or too low, and always too hard.

– Dad, you've got to hit it more softly. Be gentle, I said.
– OK, OK.

Eventually he calmed down and didn't over-hit the ball. But he had little control of the direction. The ball was going all over the place and most of the serves were faults. I could sense his frustration. 'Too bloody hard,' he said to himself. And turning to me:

– Why can't I just hit it up there on the wall? he asked, laughing a little awkwardly.

He hit a few more and they were even worse. Now they were not only lacking direction; he had returned to hitting the ball too hard.

– Let me show you again, I said.

*Learning to serve.*¹⁴²

I served a couple more sidewalls. Trying once more, he took a ball from me, lined himself up a little too quickly and served with a rushed stroke. This time he mis-hit the ball on the racket frame.

– God, what's wrong with me? he half shouted.

Anna, who was seated behind the dedans netting, looked up from her crossword and raised her eyebrows at me.

Like most people, Dad sometimes becomes frustrated and impatient. Usually it's due to the actions of another person, for instance when the driver in the car in front seems unable to make up their mind where to turn. But here, when serving on the tennis court, he was generating it himself. He became so intent on achieving the objective that each failure to do so resulted in a punishing self-critique – either verbally or in his head – that dragged him further down, destroying his confidence. By the end his service action was hurried, his concentration had disappeared, his task was near impossible. He was like the zen archery student I had read about whose failure lay in trying too hard to hit the target. Dad could control neither the ball nor himself. It was a side of my father – a man who I considered unusually composed and gentle – that I had rarely seen.

*

I decided to switch tactics and suggested we have a short game so he could put what I'd taught him into practice and experience some of the surprises, subtleties and thrills of a match. I didn't want to be like my old piano teacher who persisted in making me repeat scales over and over before allowing me to play through a whole piece.

I began at the service end, with him receiving. My first serve hit the side wall, then the penthouse and bounced on the floor. Dad was so busy watching the ball he forgot to move his feet and it bounced up awkwardly into his body. He managed to swing but the ball hit the racket frame and went into the bottom of the net. Fifteen-love. On the next serve he remembered to move, took a big swing and the ball flew up and hit the roof. Thirty-love.

– Sorry Romes, he shouted down to me.

– Nothing to be sorry about, I replied.

I then gave him an easier serve that rolled gently off the side penthouse. He returned it, quite firmly, into my forehand corner. I moved across to the ball and hit it down the middle of the court to his forehand. He mis-hit the shot but it still came back. I hit my next return so it rebounded off the main wall to his forehand; I wanted to test him with a tough shot. He took a big swing and middled it brilliantly. The ball sped cross-court and I couldn't reach it. 'Yes!' I hissed under my breath. I was elated, as if I had hit it myself. Dad was looking at me with an unfamiliar grin. Anna cheered from the dedans.

When it was Dad's turn to serve I was worried he might still feel his earlier anxiety and frustrations. But somehow, in the midst of playing the game, they had disappeared. His serves weren't perfect but they made it over. We had several good ral-

The path of my shot into the main wall and Dad's amazing winner into my backhand corner.[143]

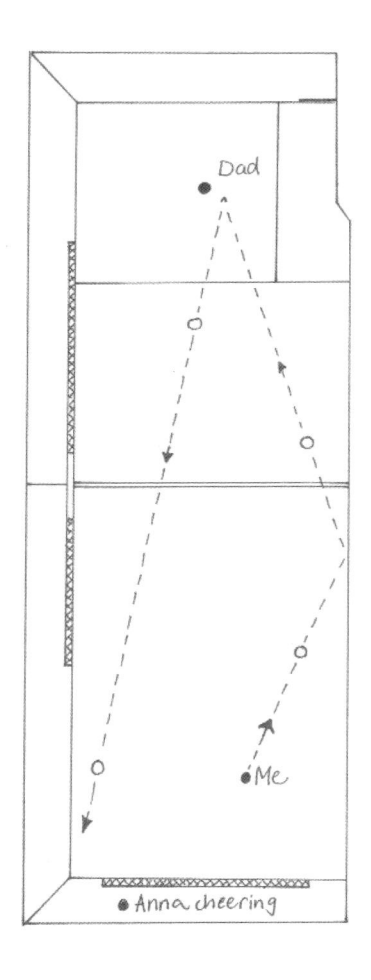

lies, with Dad's slightly wayward shots bouncing back into court off the walls or rolling around on the penthouses. During one point I hit my return cross-court to his backhand and he struck the ball parallel to the main wall. It sped down the line into the tambour, the angled buttress jutting out from the main wall. I wasn't ready for such a good shot and the ball glanced off at an unexpected angle in front of me, out of my reach. Dad was still standing in the place where he hit the ball, obviously in a state of shock.

— Your point, Dad. That's how to play tennis.

Dad looking a natural, his first time on a tennis court.[144]

— Did I do that?! I suppose I did. It really felt . . . that felt good. It's a pretty effective shot when you hit the ball into that thing, isn't it?

— Into the tambour. Yes.

— And it's obviously beneficial to be up here at the service end, because you have the tumba to aim at, and also the unicorn in the red square.

— The unicorn is called the grille, remember? And it's tambour, not tumba. Tennis is full of old French words. By the way, you're right. It's an advantage to be up the service end.

Dad was starting to understand some of the strategic complexities that make tennis unusual. He then looked up and around at the four walls surrounding us, adding:

— This is great. It's like being inside a giant pinball machine, all the walls and angles and targets and the ball flying around all over the place.

It was quite a good analogy. Perhaps I would start using it myself.

✢

I could hear the bells of the city churches chiming outside. It was noon. Two other people were waiting to come on court. Dad and I approached the net and we pushed the balls in the trough along to the net post, where they collected in the wicker basket ready for the next players. The four of us squeezed past each other in the narrow corridor and Dad and I emerged into the club room. He sat down on the sofa, sweating, red-faced, but obviously happy.

— Thanks mate . . . I missed a hell of a lot of shots. Must have had a hole in my strings!

— I think you did well, I said.

— I wasn't too bad for such an old guy. I've still got a decent eye for a ball . . . You're a good coach, mate.

— Thanks Dad.

— We could, if you want, play again next week. You know, if it would help your book . . .

I was surprised that Dad had been so agile and skilful on court. I think I'd forgotten he was a fine athlete in his youth. For some years I'd been conscious that my father was becoming an old man. Each time we met his eyes appeared a little dimmer and more watery, his memory seemed worse, he was increasingly repetitive. Now, however, I was forced to reassess him. Although he wasn't moving like a twenty-year-old, he certainly had maintained his hand-eye coordination and some physical grace. I had been too quick to condemn him to the category of 'old man'.

While Dad was proud of his performance, I had felt pride when he announced, 'you're a good coach, mate'. It wasn't that I wanted to show off to him or receive a cheap ego boost. Rather, I was seeking recognition and approval from someone I deeply cared about. I wanted him to know that I had been doing something useful with my life and the opportunities he had given me. And I wanted him to realise that I was capable of giving to other people — if only by teaching them how to play tennis or writing a book that might encourage them to be more sensitive to human suffering and other people's ways of looking at the world.

*

After getting changed, the three of us went to The Bear, a pub around the corner from the tennis court. Anna sipped at a glass of wine and I joined Dad in a midday pint. Dad wasn't saying much. He seemed to be thinking.

— There's something else, he blurted out into the silence.
— What's that, my love? said Anna.

He turned towards me.

— If I'm receiving, where's the best place to aim? Should I be trying to hit it into the corners so you can't reach it? Or is better to hit the windows on the side, or the big opening at the end of the court?
— Ah, now you're trying to steal all my secrets! It all depends on things like the score or the size of the court you're playing on. That's what makes tennis so amazing. You need the strategic mind of a chess player to be good at tennis.
— I *am* a chess player! he exclaimed.
— I know. I know. Tennis is perfect for you.
— I could be beating you pretty soon, maestro!

Dad stood up and went to refill our glasses at the bar.

— I think he's hooked, said Anna.
— I'm amazed he's so enthusiastic about it. I was starting to think that he'd spend the rest of his life playing golf and fixing the drains at home.
— Well, let's see how long it lasts. Maybe he'll be so sore tomorrow he won't be able to get out of bed. By the way, I didn't realise what a good teacher you are. I'm impressed.
— I guess I'm not bad at teaching.
— I think you've inspired your father to become a tennis fanatic! replied Anna.
— I don't really care if Dad keeps playing or not. I just want

him to realise that he can do new things, take up new challenges, have adventures.

— But maybe he doesn't want or need new adventures. Don't forget he had a pretty turbulent childhood. Perhaps stability and security are more important for him than for you.

I pondered her words for a moment, and then said:

— It's not that I think Dad should go off and climb Everest. I just want him to enjoy life while he can.

Dad returned with the drinks and the three of us began discussing where we would travel the next time they visited Europe. Would we do the usual thing and hire a cottage in Cornwall or might we venture somewhere new? Perhaps we could go camping in Cumbria or walking in the mountains in the south of Spain. Anna and I debated the options. Dad was only half-listening. He was staring intently into his pint glass. Then he spoke suddenly:

— You know, Romes, I was thinking about the day of your mother's funeral. You were only ten. Do you remember that?

— I do. I went off and played lawn tennis all afternoon during the wake, I replied.

— That's right. I think lawn tennis was a form of escape for you. You really needed it at the time.

— You're probably right.

— So I have a question for you, said Dad.

— Go ahead.

— Now you play this other kind of tennis. What does it help you escape from?

I am still searching for the answer.

Notes

1. Barcellon 1987 [1800] 41.
2. Garnett 1999, 342–344.
3. Garsault 1767, Plate 2. By permission of the Bodleian Library, University of Oxford.
4. Gillmeister 1997, 28.
5. Photo by Kate Raworth.
6. Aberdare 1980, 115.
7. Ronaldson 1985, 53.
8. Photo by Kate Raworth from a print at the Royal Tennis Court.
9. Keller 2003 [1908].
10. Ratey 2003, 178.
11. Suzuki 1973, 21; Herrigel 1985, 5.
12. Etchebaster 1971, 48.
13. Heathcote 1903, 40.
14. De Luze 1979 [1933], 71.
15. James 2000, ch. 16.
16. Huizinga 1955, 40–41.
17. Blanchard 1995, 221.
18. Gillmeister 1997, 87.
19. Gillmeister 1997, 7–9, 34.
21. Marshall 1973, 13.
20. De Hesdin and de Gonesse fol.151v. By permission of the British Library.
22. Gillmeister 1997, 32.
23. Stella and Bouzonnet-Stella (1667), Plate 27. By permission of the Bodleian Library, University of Oxford.
24. Morgan 1995, 1–2, 46–47, 55–56, 81–82, 85; Morgan 2001, 1–2.
25. Quoted in Marshall (1973, 18).
26. Marshall 1973, 4–5, 9, 34.
27. Quoted in Marshall (1973, 87).
28. Marshall 1973, 69.
29. Elias and Dunning 1986, 34; Holt 1989, 30–31.
30. Aberdare 1980, 36.
31. Bourdieu 1996, 157.
32. Blanchard 1995, 130, 178.
33. Aberdare 1980, 64.
34. Neyffer 1608, Plate 26. By permission of the Bodleian Library.
35. Gillmeister 1997, 24–25.
36. Barcellon 1987 [1800], 2.
37. Marshall 1973, 3.
38. Marshall 1973, 3.
39. Gillmeister 1997, 152.

40 Quoted in Aberdare (1980, 38). See also Marshall (1973, 19).
41 Morgan 2001, 99.
42 Marshall 1973, 76–77.
43 Marshall 1973, 78.
44 Marshall 1973, 25.
45 Marshall 1973, 98.
46 By permission of the Thyssen-Bornemisza Museum, Madrid.
47 Weckherlin 1603, fol.352r; by permission of the Obersotereichisches Landesmuseum; 'The Tennis Player', circle of Artur Davis (c. 18th century), by permission of the Tennis and Rackets Association.
48 Noel and Clark 1924, facing pages 36 and 38; Rob Fahey photo by Murray Glover.
49 Aberdare 1980, 62–63.
50 Morgan 2001, 91–94.
51 Marshall 1973, 67.
52 Morgan 2001, 6.
53 Marshall 1973, 21, 34.
54 Aberdare 1980, 68.
55 Morgan 2001, 96.
56 Morgan 2001, 127–129; Marshall 1973, 55.
57 Holt 1989, 17.
58 Veblen 1953, 183; Huizinga 1955, 51.
59 Holt 1989, 20–21, 25.
60 Barcellon 1987, 18.
61 Marshall 1973, 43.
62 Gillmeister 1997, 169n117; Marshall 1973, 45.
63 Marshall 1973, 49.
64 Marshall 1973, 105.
65 Gillmeister 1977, 174.
66 Heathcote 1903, 74–75.
67 James 2000; Blanchard 1995, 75.
68 http://www.jeremy-irons.com/film/index.html.
69 Elias and Dunning 1986, 49.
70 Elias and Dunning 1986, 41; Veblen 1953, 170.
71 Elias and Dunning 1986, 56–57.
72 Blanchard 1995, 187.
73 Blanchard 1995, 122–123.
74 Storr 1968, 118.
75 Marshall 1973, 5.
76 Marshall 1973, 42.
77 Heathcote 1903, 40–41.
78 Wade 1996, 181.
79 Whittington 2002, 242–243; Gillmeister 1997, 35; Marshall 1973, 28n2; Blanchard 1995, 103–112.
80 Totomac Civilization by Diego Rivera (1950), by permission of the Bridgeman Art Library;

NOTES

Neyffer 1608, Plate 18, by permission of the Bodleian Library, University of Oxford.
[81] Uriarte 2002, 41–49.
[82] Culin 1907, 562–563, 595.
[83] Quoted in Culin (1907, 589).
[84] Gillmeister 1997, 140–141.
[85] Gillmeister 1997, 132.
[86] 'Le Serment de Jeu de Paume, Versaille le 20 jun 1789' by Jacques Louis David (1791), by permission of of Réunion des Musées Nationaux, Paris.
[87] Schama 1989, 358–361.
[88] Garsault 1767, Plates IV and V; by permission of the Bodleian Library, University of Oxford; photos by Kate Raworth.
[89] Mastropietro and Lennox 1999, 10–12.
[90] Mastropietro and Lennox 1999, 22–24, 37–39.
[91] De Luze 1979, 71–98; Potter 1994, 61, 73; Marshall 1973 22–23, 25, 42, 84–85.
[92] Quoted in De Luze 1979, 98.
[93] Gillmeister 1997, 108–109, 115.
[94] Noel and Clark 1991, 562.
[95] Csikszentmihalyi 2000, 35–37.
[96] Huizinga 1955, 28; Blanchard 1995, 39–41; Veblen 1953, 170.
[97] Photo by Frank Baron, by permission of The Guardian.
[98] Heathcote 1903, 48.
[99] Photo by Noël Edwards.
[100] www.waynedavies.com.
[101] Best 2002, 221. Photo by Martin Bronstein, by permission of David Best.
[102] Etchebaster 1971, cover.
[103] Noel and Clark 1924, facing p65.
[104] Author photo.
[105] Garsault 1767, Plate 2, by permission of the Bodleian Library, University of Oxford.
[106] The following words are from my interview with Ben Ronaldson.
[107] Etchebaster 1971, xviii–xix.
[108] Etchebaster 1971, 9–13.
[109] The archer's words are adapted from Herrigel (1985, 5–6, 14–15, 63–64).
[110] Marshall 1973, 1.
[111] Noel and Clark 1924, 285.
[112] Orwell 1977, 108.
[113] Quoted in De Botton 2004, 144.

NOTES

[114] Photo by Noël Edwards.
[115] Holt 1989, 98–100.
[116] Aberdare 1933, facing p157.
[117] Aberdare 1980, 298
[118] Quoted in Dawes (1973, 12).
[119] Orwell 1977, 68.
[120] Orwell 1977, 68–69.
[121] Dawes, 1973, 11.
[122] Barrie 1916, 5, 34.
[123] Photos by Kate Raworth.
[124] Wade 1996, 66.
[125] James 2000, 171.
[126] Chris Ronaldson personal collection; photo by Kate Raworth.
[127] Lesley Ronaldson personal collection; photo by Kate Raworth.
[128] Ronaldson 1985, 95.
[129] Photo by Martin Bronstein, by permission of David Best.
[130] Best 2002, 140.
[131] Howell 1995, 21.
[132] *Tennis* magazine, November 1990, No. 101 (West of England Newspapers, Plymouth, UK).
[133] Off-court photo by Brian Dowling. On-court photo by Maynard Hall.
[134] Best 2002, 168. Photo of the 1999 Dresdner Kleinwort Benson tournament contestants, by permission of David Best.
[135] 'St John the Evangelist' by El Greco, by permission of the Prado Musuem, Madrid; Chris Ronaldson photo by Kate Raworth.
[136] Guillaume Barcellon, tennis professional to Louis XV by Etienne Loys (1753), by permission of the Wimbledon Lawn Tennis Museum.
[137] Barcellon 1987, 33.
[138] Heathcote 1903, 40.
[139] Photo by Kate Raworth.
[140] Drawing by Kate Raworth.
[141] Drawing by Kate Raworth.
[142] Photo by Kate Raworth.
[143] Drawing by Kate Raworth.
[144] Photo by Kate Raworth.

References

Aberdare, Lord (1980) *The Willis Faber Book of Tennis & Rackets*, Stanley Paul (London).

Aberdare, Lord et al (eds) (1933) *Rackets, Squash Rackets, Tennis, Fives and Badminton*, The Lonsdale Library Volume XVI, Seeley Service & Co. (London).

Barcellon, Pierre (1987 [1800]) *Rules and Principles of Tennis*, translated by Sir Richard Hamilton, Bt., Ironbark, Ronaldson Publications (Oxford).

Barrie, J.M. (1916) *The Admirable Crichton*, Hodder & Staughton (London).

Best, David (2002) *The Royal Tennis Court: A History of Tennis at Hampton Court Palace*, Ironbark, Ronaldson Publications (Oxford).

Blanchard, Kendall (1995) *The Anthropology of Sport: An Introduction*, Bergin & Garvey (Westport, CT).

Bourdieu, Pierre (1996) 'Programme For a Sociology of Sport' in *In Other Words: Essays Towards a Reflexive Sociology*, Polity Press (Cambridge).

Csikszentmihalyi, Mihalyi (2000) *Beyond Boredom and Anxiety: Experiencing Flow in Work and Play*, Jossey-Bass Publishers (San Francisco).

Culin, Stewart (1907) *Games of the North American Indians*, Bureau of American Ethnology, Government Printing Office (Washington).

Dawes, Frank (1973) *Not in Front of the Servants: Domestic Service in*

REFERENCES

England 1850–1939, Wayland Publishers (London).

De Botton, Alain (2004) *Status Anxiety*, Hamish Hamilton (London).

Disley, John (ed) (1996) 'A Life of Brian' (privately printed, Leamington Spa, 70 pages).

Elias, Norbert and Eric Dunning (1986) *Quest For Excitement: Sport and Leisure in the Civilizing Process*, Blackwell (Oxford).

Etchebaster, Pierre (1971) *Pierre's Book: The Game of Court Tennis*, Barre Publishers (Barre, MA).

Garnett, Michael P. 1999: *'A Chase Down-Under' – A History of Royal Tennis in Australia*, Historical Publications (Romsey, Victoria).

de Garsault, M. (1767) *Art du Paumier-Raquetier et de la Paume* (Paris).

Gillmeister, Heiner (1997) *Tennis: A Cultural History*, Leicester University Press (London).

Heathcote, J. M. (1903) Tennis, in *The Badminton Library of Sports and Pastimes: Tennis, Lawn Tennis, Rackets, Fives*, Longmans (London).

Herrigel, Eugen (1985) *Zen in the Art of Archery*, Arkana (London).

de Hesdin, Simon and Nicolas de Gonesse (c. 15th century) *Valerius Maximus*, Harley 4375, British Library (London).

Holt, Richard (1989) *Sport and the British: A Modern History*, Clarendon Press (Oxford).

Howell, Jonathan (1995) *More Than A Yard Worse*, Ironbark, Ronaldson Publications (Oxford).

Huizinga, Johan (1955) *Homo Ludens: A Study of the Play Element in Culture*, The Beacon Press (Boston).

REFERENCES

James, C.L.R. (2000) *Beyond a Boundary*, Serpent's Tail (London).

Keller, Helen (2003 [1908]) *The World I Live In*, New York Review of Books (New York).

de Luze, Albert (1979 [1933]) *A History of the Royal Game of Tennis*, translator Richard Hamilton, Roundwood Press (Warwickhire).

Marshall, Julian (1973 [1878]) *The Annals of Tennis*, Racket Sports Information and Services (Baltimore).

Mastropeitro, Stefano and Tim Lennox (1999) 'Design of Real Tennis Balls', Cambridge University Engineering Department Report No. 33/2503, in association with Alfred Reader and Company, Teston, and Cambridge University Real Tennis Club.

McNicoll, Kathryn (2005) *Real Tennis*, Shire Publications (Princes Risborough, Buckinghamshire).

Morgan, Roger (2001) *Tudor Tennis: A Miscellany*, Ironbark, Ronaldson Publications (Oxford).

Morgan, Roger (1995) *Tennis: The Development of the European Ball Game*, Ironbark, Ronaldson Publications (Oxford).

Neyffer, Johann Christoph (1608) *Illustrissimi Wirtembergici Ducalis novi Collegii*, Bodleian Library (Oxford).

Noel, E B. and J.O.M. Clark (1924) *A History of Tennis*, Oxford University Press (Oxford).

Orwell, George (1977) *Down and Out in Paris and London*, Penguin (Harmondsworth).

Potter, Jeremy (1994) *Tennis and Oxford*, Oxford Unicorn Press (Oxford).

Ratey, John (2003) *A User's Guide to the Brain*, Abacus (London).

REFERENCES

Ronaldson, Chris (1985) *Tennis: A Cut Above The Rest*, Ironbark, Ronaldson Publications (Oxford).

Schama, Simon (1989) *Citizens: A Chronicle of the French Revolution*, Viking (London).

Stella, Jacques and Claudine Bouzonnet-Stella (1667) *Les jeux et les plaisirs de l'enfance*, Editions Slatkine (Paris).

Storr, Anthony (1968) *Human Aggression*, Allen Lane, The Penguin Press (London).

Suzuki, Shunryu (1973) *Zen Mind, Beginner's Mind*, Weatherhill (New York and Tokyo).

Uriarte, María Teresa (2002) 'Unity in Duality: The Practice and Symbols of the Mesoamerican Ballgame' in E. Michael Whittington (ed), *The Sport of Life and Death: The Mesoamerican Ballgame*, Mint Museum of Art (Charlotte, North Carolina) and Thames & Hudson.

Veblen, Thorsten (1953) *The Theory of the Leisure Class*, Mentor (New York).

Wade, Charles (1996) *The History of the Leamington Tennis Court Club 1846–1996*, Ironbark, Ronaldson Publications (Oxford).

Weckherlin, Michael (1603) *Wappenbuch*, MS 10, 737, Oberosterreichisches Landesmuseum (Linz).

Whittington, E. Michael (ed) (2002) *The Sport of Life and Death: The Mesoamerican Ballgame*, Mint Museum of Art (Charlotte, North Carolina) and Thames & Hudson.

Acknowledgements

Bertrand Faure-Beaulieu provided essential funding for the research, which made it possible to complete a project I had begun in 1998. I would also like to give special thanks to William Alden, Managing Director of the Alden Group and a member of the Oxford University Tennis Club, for his generous financial support for the printing of this book. Kathryn McNicoll from Ronaldson Publications was an enthusiastic and wise editor. Sam Davies designed the book with a sensitive and creative eye.

Many tennis players – most of them professionals – were willing to share their thoughts and experiences in recorded interviews. They included: Brian Church, Wayne Davies, Jon Dawes, Peter Dawes, Lachlan Deuchar, Kees Ludekens, Alan Oliver, Ben Ronaldson, Chris Ronaldson, Lesley Ronaldson, Kevin Sheldon and Julian Snow. Marion Haberhauer and Sophia Blackwell did excellent transcriptions of these interviews.

Over the years dozens of other players have also talked with me about what tennis means to them. I hope they don't mind that I kept notes.

At the Oxford University Tennis Club, Freddy Adam, Andrew Davis, Alan Oliver, Nicolas Victoir, Rob Walker and Spike Willcocks tolerated my regular rants on tennis and the meaning of life.

Several historians and scholars of the game gave me guidance, access to their research materials and copies of unpublished work, amongst them: Thierry Bernard-Tambour, Cees de Bondt, Heiner Gillmeister, Roger Morgan and Brian Rich. I also received much assistance from librarians at the

ACKNOWLEDGEMENTS

Bodleian in Oxford, the Cambridge University Library and the British Library. Special thanks also to Gerard J. Belliveau, Jr., Librarian at The Racquet and Tennis Club in New York.

Revan Schendler inspired me to begin working on this book and helped me to understand the importance of looking beneath the surface of things.

Theodore Zeldin encouraged me to describe the beauty in tennis and provided enlightening comments on the manuscript.

I shared thoughts with, and received advice from, many friends, including: Geoff Baker, Flora Gathorne-Hardy, Lisa Gormley, Eric Lonergan, Eka Morgan, Richard Raworth, Andrew Ray, John Reed, Colin Ward, Harriet Ward, Andy Whitmore and Andrew Wroe.

And to follow that peculiar convention where the most important person is mentioned last, there is Kate Raworth. She read countless drafts, drew most of the pictures, took the photos, shook me out of sombre moods and academic language, and provided words when I could not find them.

The publisher is grateful to the following for permission to reproduce photos and illustrations: David Best, the Bodleian Library, University of Oxford, the Bridgeman Art Library, the British Library, Martin Bronstein, Brian Dowling, Noël Edwards, Murray Glover, The Guardian, Maynard Hall, Oberostereichisches Landesmuseum, Linz, the Prado Museum, Madrid, Kate Raworth, Réunion des Musées Nationaux, Paris, Chris Ronaldson, Lesley Ronaldson, the Royal Tennis Court, the Tennis & Rackets Association, the Thyssen-Bornemisza Museum, Madrid, and the Wimbledon Lawn Tennis Museum.

About the author

Roman Krznaric grew up in Sydney and Hong Kong, then studied at the universities of Oxford, London and Essex, where he wrote a doctoral thesis on how wealthy people think about poverty. After a period as a journalist in London and Madrid, he did human rights work in Central America with refugees and indigenous people. He taught sociology and politics at Cambridge University and City University, London. He currently works at The Oxford Muse, a foundation established by the historian Theodore Zeldin to reinvent the art of living.

Apart from scholarly publications, he is co-editor of *Guide to an Unknown University*. A selection of his other writings is available at www.romankrznaric.com.

A fanatical real tennis player for over fifteen years, he is one of the top amateur players in the world. In 2005 he won the Premier Division of the British National League, partnering the reigning World Champion, Rob Fahey. His other passions include furniture making and growing things.